The Illustrated
KAMA SUTRA

Vatsyayana • Pichard

Volume 2

The Illustrated
KAMA SUTRA
Volume 2

Georges Pichard
Vatsyayana

Translated by Sir Richard Burton
and F.F. Arbuthnot

·EUROTICA·

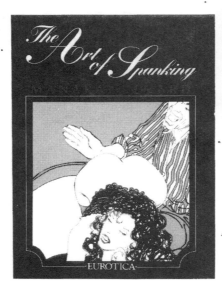

Add $2 P&H first item,
$1 each addt'l.
Write for our complete catalog:
NBM
185 Madison Ave., Ste. 1504
New York, NY 10016

ISBN 1-56163-020-9
© Editions Dominique Leroy 1991
© NBM for presentation & introduction 1991

10   9   8   7   6   5   4   3   2

Eurotica is an imprint of

NANTIER · BEALL · MINOUSTCHINE
Publishing inc.
new york

Part Three

About the Acquisition of a Wife

Chapter One

ON MARRIAGE

When a girl of the same caste, and a virgin, is married in accordance with the precepts of Holy Writ (Dharma Shastras), the results of such a union are: the acquisition of Dharma and Artha, offspring, affinity, increase of friends, and untarnished love. For this reason a man should fix his affections upon a girl who is of good family, whose parents are alive, and who is three years or more younger than himself. She should be born of a highly respectable family, possessed of wealth, well connected, and with many relations and friends. She should also be beautiful, of a good disposition, with lucky marks on her body, and with good hair, nails, teeth, ears, eyes, and breasts, neither more nor less than they ought to be, and no one of them entirely wanting, and not troubled with a sickly body. The man should, of course, also possess these qualities himself. But at all events, says Ghotaka-mukha, a girl who has been already joined with others (that is, no longer a maiden) should never be loved, for it would be reproachful to do such a thing.

Now, in order to bring about a marriage with a girl such as described above, the parents and relations of the man should exert themselves, as should such friends on both sides as may be desired to assist in the matter. These friends should bring to the notice of the girl's parents the faults, both present and future, of all the other men that may wish to marry her, and should at the same time extoll even to exaggeration all the excellences, ancestral and paternal, of their friend, so as to endear him to them, and particularly to those that may be liked by the girl's mother. One of the friends should also disguise himself as an astrologer, and declare the future good fortune and wealth of his friend by showing the existence of all the lucky omens[1] and signs,[2] the good influence of planets, the auspicious entrance of the sun into a sign of the Zodiac, propitious stars and fortunate marks on his body. Others again should rouse the jealousy of the girl's mother by telling her that their friend has a chance of getting from some other quarter an even better girl than hers.

A girl should be taken as a wife, and given in marriage, when fortune, signs, omens, and the words[3] of others are favorable, for, says Ghotakamukha, a man should not marry at any time he likes. A girl who is asleep, crying, or gone out of the house when sought in marriage, or who is betrothed to another, should not be married. The following should also be avoided:

One who is kept concealed
One who has an ill-sounding name
One who has her nose depressed
One who has her nostril turned up
One who is formed like a male
One who is bent down
One who has crooked thighs
One who has a projecting forehead
One who has a bald head
One who does not like purity
One who has been polluted by another
One who is affected with the Gulma[4]
One who is disfigured in any way
One who has fully arrived at puberty
One who is a friend
One who is a younger sister
One who is a Varshakari[5]

In the same way a girl who is called by the name of one of the twenty-seven stars, or by the name of a tree, or of a river, is considered worthless, as also a girl whose name ends in "r" or "l." But some authors say that prosperity is gained only by marrying that girl to whom one becomes attached and that therefore no other girl but the one who is loved should be married by anyone.

When a girl becomes marriageable her parents should dress her smartly, and should place her where she can be easily seen by all. Every afternoon, having dressed her and decorated her in a becoming manner, they should send her with her female companions to sports, sacrifices, and marriage ceremonies, and thus show her to advantage in society, because she is a kind of merchandise. They should also receive with kind words and signs of friendliness those of an auspicious appearance who may come accompanied by their friends and relatives for the purpose of marrying the daughter; and, under some pretext or other having first dressed her becomingly, the parents should then present her to them. After this, they should await the pleasure of fortune, and with this object should appoint a future day on which a determination could be come to with regard to their daughter's marriage. On this occasion when the persons have come, the parents of the girl should ask them to bathe and dine, and should say, "Everything will take place at the proper time," and should not then comply with the request, but should settle the matter later.

When a girl is thus acquired, either according to the custom of the country or according to his own desire, the man should marry her in accordance with the precepts of the Holy Writ, according to one of the four kinds of marriage.

Thus ends the discourse of marriage.

There are also some verses on the subject, as follows:
"Amusement in society, such as completing verses begun by others, marriages, and auspicious ceremonies, should be carried on neither with superiors nor with inferiors, but with our equals. That should be known as a high connection when a man, after marrying a girl, has to serve her and her relatives afterward like a servant, and such a connection is censured by the good. On the other hand, that reproachable connection where a man, together with his relatives, lords it over his wife is called a low connection by the wise. But when both the man and the woman afford mutual pleasure to each other, and where the relatives on both sides pay respect to one another, such is called a connection in the proper sense of the word. Therefore a man should contract neither a high connection by which he is obliged to bow down afterward to his kinsmen, nor a low connection, which is universally reprehended by all."

[1] The flight of a bluejay on a person's left is considered a lucky omen when one starts on any business; the appearance of a cat before anyone at such a time is looked on as a bad omen. There are many omens of the same kind.

[2] Such as the throbbing of the right eye of men and the left eye of women, etc.

[3] Before anything is begun it is a custom to go early in the morning to a neighbor's house, and overhear the first words that may be spoken by his family, and according as the words heard are of good or bad import, so draw an inference as to the success or failure of the undertaking.

[4] A disease consisting of any glandular enlargement in any part of the body.

[5] A women the palms of whose hands and the soles of whose feet are always perspiring.

Chapter Two

ON CREATING CONFIDENCE IN THE GIRL

For the first three days after marriage, the girl and her husband should sleep on the floor, abstain from sexual pleasures, and eat their food without seasoning it either with alkali or salt. For the next seven days they should bathe amidst the sounds of auspicious musical instruments, should decorate themselves, dine together, and pay attention to their relatives as well as to those who may have come to witness their marriage. This is applicable to persons of all castes. On the night of the tenth day the man should begin in a lonely place with soft words, and thus create confidence in the girl. Some authors say that for the purpose of winning her over he should not speak to her for three days; but the followers of Babhravya are of the opinion that, if the man does not speak with her for three days, the girl may be discouraged by seeing him spiritless, like a pillar, and, becoming dejected, she may begin to despise him as a eunuch. Vatsyayana says that the man should begin to win her over, and to create confidence in her, but should abstain at first from sexual pleasures. Women being of a tender nature, want tender beginnings, and when they are forcibly approached by men with whom they are but slightly acquainted, they sometimes suddenly become haters of sexual connection, and sometimes even haters of the male sex. The man should therefore approach the girl according to her liking, and should make use of those devices by which he may be able to establish himself more and more in her confidence. These devices are as follows:

He should embrace her first of all in the way she likes most, because it does not last for a long time.

He should embrace her with the upper part of his body, because that is easier and simpler. If the girl is grown up, or if the man has known her for some time, he may embrace her by the light of a lamp; but if he is not well acquainted with her, or if she is a young girl, he should then embrace her in darkness.

When the girl accepts the embrace, the man should put a "tambula," or screw of betel nut and betel leaves, in her mouth, and if she will not take it, he should induce her to do so by conciliatory words, entreaties, oaths, and kneeling at her feet, for it is a universal rule that, however bashful or angry a woman may be, she never disregards a man's kneeling at her feet. At the time of giving this tambula, he should kiss her mouth softly and gracefully, without making any sound. When she is gained over in this respect, he should then make her talk, and so that she may be induced to talk he should ask her questions about things of which he knows or pretends to know nothing, and which can be answered in a few words. If she does not speak to him, he should not frighten her, but should ask her the same thing again and again in a conciliatory manner. If she does not then speak, he should urge her to give a reply because, as Ghotakamukha says, "All girls hear everything said to them by men, but do not themselves sometimes say a single word." When she is thus importuned, the girl should give replies by shakes of the head, but if she quarreled with the man she should not even do that. When she is asked by the man whether she desires him, and whether she likes him, she should remain silent for a long time, and when at last importuned to reply, should give him a favorable answer by a nod of her head. If the man is previously acquainted with the girl, he should converse with her by means of a female friend, who may be favorable to him, and in the confidence of both, and carry on the conversation on both sides. On such an occasion the girl should smile with her head bent down, and if the female friend say more on her part than she was desired to, she should chide her and dispute with her. The female friend should say in jest even what she is not desired to say by the girl, and add, "She says so"; on which the girl should say, indistinctly and prettily, "Oh, no! I did not say so," and she should then smile, and throw an occasional glance toward the man.

If the girl is familiar with the man, she should place near him, without saying anything, the tambula, the ointment, or the garland that he may have asked for, or she may tie them up in his upper garment. While she is engaged in this, the man should touch her young breasts in the sounding way of pressing with the nails, and if she prevents him doing this he should say to her, "I will not do it again if you will embrace me," and should in this way cause her to embrace him. While he is being embraced by her he should pass his hand repeatedly over and about her body. By and by he should place her in his lap, and try more and more to gain her consent, and if she will not yield to him he should frighten her by saying: "I shall impress marks of my teeth and nails on your lips and breasts, and then make similar marks on my own body, and shall tell my friends that you did them. What will you say then?" In this and other ways, as fear and confidence are created in the minds of children, so should the man gain her over to his wishes.

On the second and third nights, after her confidence has increased still more, he should feel the whole of her body with his hands, and kiss her all over; he should also place his hands upon her thighs and shampoo them, and if he succeeds in this he should then shampoo the joints of her thighs. If she tries to prevent him doing this, he should say to her, "What harm is there in doing it?" and should persuade her to let him do it. After gaining this point he should touch her private parts, should loosen her girdle and the knot of her dress, and, turning up her lower garment, should shampoo the joints of her naked thighs. Under various pretenses he should do all these things, but he should not at that time begin actual congress. After this, he should teach her the sixty-four arts, should tell her how much he loves her, and describe to her the hopes he formerly entertained regarding her. He should also promise to be faithful to her in the future, and should dispel all her fears with respect to rival women, and at last, after having overcome her bashfulness, he should begin to enjoy her in a way so as not to frighten her. So much about creating confidence in the girl; there are, moreover, some verses on the subject, as follows:

"A man acting according to the inclinations of a girl should try to gain her over so that she may love him and place her confidence in him. A man does not succeed either by implicitly following the inclination of a girl or by wholly opposing her, and he should therefore adopt a middle course. He who knows how to make himself beloved by women, as well as to increase their honor and create confidence in them, becomes an object of their love. But he who neglects a girl, thinking she is too bashful, is despised by her as a beast ignorant of the working of the female mind. Moreover, a girl forcibly enjoyed by one who does not understand the hearts of girls becomes nervous, uneasy, and dejected, and suddenly begins to hate the man who has taken advantage of her; and then, when her love is not understood or returned, she sinks into despondency, and becomes either a hater of mankind altogether or, hating her own man, she has recourse to other men."[1]

[1] The last few lines have been exemplified in many ways in many novels of this century.

Chapter Three

ON COURTSHIP, AND THE MANIFESTATION OF THE FEELINGS BY OUTWARD SIGNS AND DEEDS

A poor man possessed of good qualities, a man born of a low family possessed of mediocre qualities, a neighbor possessed of wealth, and one under the control of his father, mother, or brothers, should not marry without endeavoring to gain over the girl from her childhood to love and esteem them. Thus a boy separated from his parents, and living in the house of his uncle, should try to gain over the daughter of his uncle, or some other girl, even though she be previously betrothed to another. And this way of gaining over a girl, says Ghotakamukha, is unexceptionable, because Dharma can be accomplished by means of it, as well as by any other way of marriage.

When a boy has thus begun to woo the girl he loves, he should spend his time with her and amuse her with various games and diversions fitted for their age and acquaintanceship, such as picking and collecting flowers, making garlands of flowers, playing the parts of members of a fictitious family, cooking food, playing with dice, playing with cards, the game of odd and even, the game of finding out the middle finger, the game of six pebbles, and such other games as may be prevalent in the country, and agreeable to the disposition of the girl. In addition to this, he should carry on various amusing games played by several persons together, such as hide-and-seek, playing with seeds, hiding things in several small heaps of wheat and looking for them, blind-man's buff, gymnastic exercises, and other games of the same sort in company with the girl, her friends, and female attendants. The man should also show great kindness to any woman whom the girl thinks fit to be trusted, and should also make new acquaintances, but above all he should attach to himself by kindness and little services the daughter of the girl's nurse, for if she be gained over, even though she comes to know of his design, she does not cause any obstruction, but is sometimes even able to effect a union between him and the girl. And though she knows the true character of the man, she always talks of his many excellent qualities to the parents and relations of the girl, even though she may not be desired to do so by him.

In this way the man should do whatever the girl takes most delight in, and he should get for her whatever she may have a desire to possess. Thus he should procure for her such playthings as may be hardly known to other girls. He may also show her a ball dyed with various colors, and other curiosities of the same sort; and should give her dolls made of cloth, wood, buffalo horn, ivory, wax, flour, or earth; also utensils for cooking food; and figures in wood, such as a man and woman standing, a pair of rams or goats or sheep; also temples made of earth, bamboo, or wood, dedicated to various goddesses, and cages for parrots, cuckoos, starlings, quails, cocks, and partridges; water vessels of different sorts and of elegant forms, machines for throwing water about, guitars, stands for putting images upon, stools, lac, red arsenic, yellow ointment, vermilion and collyrium, as well as sandalwood, saffron, betel nut and betel leaves. Such things should be given at different times whenever he gets a good opportunity of meeting her in public, according to circumstances. In short, he should try in every way to make her look upon him as one who would do for her everything that she wanted to be done.

In the next place he should get her to meet him in some place privately, and should then tell her that the reason for his giving presents to her in secret was the fear that the parents of both of them might be displeased, and then he may add that the things which he had given her had been much desired by other people. When her love begins to show signs of increasing, he should relate to her agreeable stories if she expresses a wish to hear such narratives. Or if she takes delight in legerdemain, he should amaze her by performing various tricks of jugglery; or if she feels a great curiosity to see a performance of the various arts, he should show his own skill in them. When she is delighted with singing, he should entertain her with music, and on certain days, and at the time of going together to moonlight fairs and festivals, and at the time of her return after being absent from home, he should present her with bouquets of flowers and with chaplets for the head and with ear ornaments and rings, for these are the proper occasions on which such things should be presented.

He should also teach the daughter of the girl's nurse all the sixty-four means of pleasure practiced by men, and under this pretext should also inform her of his great skill in the art of sexual enjoyment. All this time he should wear a fine dress, and make as good an appearance as possible, for young women love men who live with them, and who are handsome, good looking, and well dressed. As for the saying that, though women may fall in love, they still make no effort themselves to gain over the object of their affections, that is only a matter of idle talk.

Now, a girl always shows her love by outward signs and actions such as the following:
She never looks the man in the face, and becomes abashed when she is looked at by him; under some pretext or other she shows her limbs to him; she looks secretly at him, though he has gone away from her side; hangs down her head when she is asked some question by him, and answers in indistinct words and unfinished sentences, delights to be in his company for a long time, speaks to her attendants in a peculiar tone with the hope of attracting his attention toward her when she is at a distance from him, and does not wish to go from the place where he is; under some pretext or other she makes him look at different things, narrates to him tales and stories very slowly so that she may continue conversing with him for a long time; kisses and embraces before him a child sitting in her lap; draws ornamental marks on the foreheads of her female servants; performs sportive and graceful movements when her attendants speak jestingly to her in the presence of her lover; confides in her lover's friends, and respects and obeys them; shows kindness to his servants, converses with them and engages them to do her work as if she were their mistress, and listens attentively to them when they tell stories about her lover to somebody else; enters his house when induced to do so by the daughter of her nurse, and by her assistance manages to converse and play with him; avoids being seen by her lover when she is not dressed and decorated; gives him by the hand of her female friend her ear ornament, ring, or garland of flowers that he may have asked to see; always wears anything that he may have presented to her; becomes dejected when any other bridegroom is mentioned by her parents, and does not mix with those who may be of his party, or who may support his claims.

There are also some verses on the subject, as follows:
"A man who has seen and perceived the feelings of the girl toward him, and who has noticed the outward signs and movements by which those feelings are expressed, should do everything in his power to effect a union with her. He should gain over a young girl by childlike sports; a damsel come of age by his skill in the arts; and a girl that loves him by having recourse to persons in whom she confides."

Chapter Four

ON THINGS TO BE DONE ONLY BY THE MAN, AND THE ACQUISITION OF THE GIRL THEREBY. ALSO, WHAT IS TO BE DONE BY A GIRL TO GAIN OVER A MAN, AND SUBJECT HIM TO HER

Now, when the girl begins to show her love by outward signs and motions, as described in the last chapter, the lover should try to gain her over entirely by various ways and means, such as the following:

When engaged with her in any game or sport, he should intentionally hold her hand. He should practice upon her the various kinds of embraces, such as the touching embrace, and others already described in a preceding chapter (Part Two, Chapter II). He should show her a pair of human beings cut out of the leaf of a tree, and suchlike things, at intervals. When engaged in water sports, he should dive at a distance from her, and come up close to her. He should show an increased liking for the new foliage of trees and suchlike things. He should describe to her the pangs he suffers on her account. He should relate to her the beautiful dream that he has had with reference to other women. At parties and assemblies of his caste he should sit near her, and touch her under some pretense or other and, having placed his foot upon hers, he should slowly touch each of her toes, and press the ends of the nails; if successful in this, he should get hold of her foot with his hand and repeat the same thing. He should also press a finger of her hand between his toes when she happens to be washing his feet; and whenever he gives anything to her or takes anything from her, he should show her by his manner and looks how much he loves her.

He should sprinkle upon her the water brought for rinsing his mouth; and when alone with her in a lonely place, or in darkness, he should make love to her, and tell her the true state of his mind without distressing her in any way.

Whenever he sits with her on the same seat or bed he should say to her, "I have something to tell you in private," and then, when she comes to hear it in a quiet place, he should express his love to her more by manner and signs than by words. When he comes to know the state of her feelings toward him, he should pretend to be ill, and should make her come to his house to speak to him. There he should intentionally hold her hand and place it on his eyes and forehead, and under the pretense of preparing some medicine for him he should ask her to do the work for his sake in the following words: "This work must be done by you, and by nobody else." When she wants to go away he should let her go, with an earnest request to come and see him again. This device of illness should be continued for three days and three nights. After this, when she begins coming to see him frequently, he should carry on long conversations with her, for, says Ghotakamukha, "though a man loves a girl ever so much, he never succeeds in winning her without a great deal of talking." At last, when the man finds the girl completely won over, he may then begin to enjoy her. As for the saying that women grow less timid than usual during the evening, at night, and in darkness, and are desirous of congress at those times, and do not oppose men then, and should only be enjoyed at these hours, it is a matter of talk only.

When it is impossible for the man to carry on his endeavors alone, he should, by means of the daughter of her nurse, or of a female friend in whom she confides, cause the girl to be brought to him without making known to her his design, and he should then proceed with her in the manner above described. Or he should in the beginning send his own female servant to live with the girl as her friend, and should then gain her over by her means.

At last, when he knows the state of her feeling by her outward manner and conduct toward him at religious ceremonies, marriage ceremonies, fairs, festivals, theaters, public assemblies, and suchlike occasions, he should begin to enjoy her when she is alone, for Vatsyayana lays it down that women, when resorted to at proper times and in proper places, do not turn away from their lovers.

When a girl, possessed of good qualities and well bred, though born of a humble family, or destitute of wealth, and not therefore desired by her equals, or an orphan girl, or one deprived of her parents, but observing the rules of her family and caste, wishes to bring about her own marriage when she comes of age, such a girl should endeavor to gain over a strong and good-looking young man or a person whom she thinks would marry her on account of the weakness of his mind, and even without the consent of his parents. She should do this by such means as would endear her to the said person, as well as by frequently seeing and meeting him. Her mother also should constantly cause them to meet by means of her female friends, and the daughter of her nurse. The girl herself should try to get alone with her beloved in some quiet place, and at odd times should give him flowers, betel nut, betel leaves, and perfumes. She should also show her skill in the practice of the arts, in shampooing, in scratching and in pressing with the nails. She should also talk to him on the subjects he likes best, and discuss with him the ways and means of gaining over and winning the affections of a girl.

But old authors say that, although the girl loves the man ever so much, she should not offer herself, or make the first overtures, for a girl who does this loses her dignity, and is liable to be scorned and rejected. But when the man shows his wish to enjoy her, she should be favorable to him, and should show no change in her demeanor when he embraces her, and should receive all the manifestations of his love as if she were ignorant of the state of his mind. But when he tries to kiss her she should oppose him; when he begs to be allowed to have sexual intercourse with her, she should let him touch her private parts only and with considerable difficulty; and though importuned by him, she should not yield herself up to him as if of her own accord, but should resist his attempts to have her.

Moreover, it is only when she is certain that she is truly loved and that her lover is indeed devoted to her, and will not change his mind, that she should then give herself up to him, and persuade him to marry her quickly. After losing her virginity she should tell her confidential friends about it.

Here ends discourse of the efforts of a girl to gain over a man.

There are also some verses on the subject, as follows:

"A girl who is much sought after should marry the man she likes, and whom she thinks would be obedient to her, and capable of giving her pleasure. But when from the desire of wealth a girl is married by her parents to a rich man without taking into consideration the character or looks of the bridegroom, or when given to a man who has several wives, she never becomes attached to the man, even though he be endowed with good qualities, obedient to her will, active, strong, and healthy, and anxious to please her in every way.[1] A husband who is obedient but yet master of himself, though he be poor and not good looking, is better than one who is common to many women, even though he be handsome and attractive. The wives of rich men, where there are many wives, are not generally attached to their husbands, and are not confidential with them, even though they possess all the external enjoyments of life, still have recourse to other men. A man who is of a low mind, who has fallen from his social position, and who is much given to traveling, does not deserve to be married; neither does one who has many wives and children, or one who is devoted to sport and gambling, and who comes to his wife only when he likes. Of all the lovers of a girl, he only is her true husband who possesses the qualities that are liked by her, and such a husband enjoys real superiority over her only because he is the husband of love."

---

[1] There is a good deal of truth in the last few observations. Woman is a monogamous animal, and loves but one, and likes to feel herself alone in the affections of one man, and cannot bear rivals. It may also be taken as a general rule that women either married to, or kept by, rich men love them for their wealth, but not for themselves.

Chapter Five

ON CERTAIN FORMS OF MARRIAGE

When a girl cannot meet her lover frequently in private, she should send the daughter of her nurse to him, it being understood that she has confidence in her, and had previously gained her over to her interests. On seeing the man, the daughter of the nurse should, in the course of conversation, describe to him the noble birth, the good disposition, the beauty, talent, skill, knowledge of human nature, and affection of the girl in such a way as not to let him suppose that she had been sent by the girl, and should thus create affection for the girl in the heart of the man. To the girl also she should speak about the excellent qualities of the man, especially of those qualities which she knows are pleasing to the girl. She should, moreover, speak with disparagement of the other lovers of the girl, and talk about the avarice and indiscretion of their parents, and the fickleness of their relations. She should also quote samples of many girls of ancient times, such as Sakuntala and others who, having united themselves with lovers of their own caste and their own choice, were happy ever afterward in their society. She should also tell of other girls who married into great families, and being troubled by rival wives became wretched and miserable, and were finally abandoned. She should further speak of the good fortune, the continual happiness, the chastity, obedience, and affection of the man; and if the girl gets amorous about him, she should endeavor to allay her shame[1] and her fear, as well as her suspicions about any disaster that might result from her marriage. In a word, she should act the whole part of a female messenger by telling the girl all about the man's affection for her, the places he frequented, and the endeavors he made to meet her, and by frequently repeating, "It will be all right if the man takes you away forcibly and unexpectedly."

The Forms of Marriage[2]

When the girl is gained over, and acts openly with the man as his wife, he should cause fire to be brought from the house of a Brahman and, having spread the Kusha grass upon the ground, and offered an oblation to the fire, he should marry her according to the precepts of the religious law. After this he should inform his parents of the fact, because it is the opinion of ancient authors that a marriage solemnly contracted in the presence of fire cannot afterward be set aside.

After the consummation of the marriage, the relations of the man should gradually be made acquainted with the affair, and the relations of the girl should also be apprised of it in such a way that they may consent to the marriage, and overlook the manner in which it was brought about, and when this is done they should afterward be reconciled by affectionate presents and favorable conduct. In this manner the man should marry the girl according to the Gandharva form of marriage.

When the girl cannot make up her mind, or will not express her readiness to marry, the man should obtain her in any one of the following ways:

(1). On a fitting occasion, and under some excuse, he should, by means of a female friend with whom he is well acquainted and whom he can trust, and who also is well known to the girl's family, get the girl brought unexpectedly to his house, and he should then bring fire from the house of a Brahman, and proceed as before described.

(2). When the marriage of the girl with some other person draws near, the man should disparage the future husband to the utmost in the mind of the mother of the girl, and then, having got the girl to come with her mother's consent to a neighboring house, he should bring fire from the house of a Brahman, and proceed as above.

(3). The man should become a great friend of the brother of the girl, the said brother being of the same age as himself, and addicted to courtesans and to intrigues with the wives of other people, and should give him assistance in such matters, and also give him occasional presents. He should then tell him about his great love for his sister, as young men will sacrifice even their lives for the sake of those who may be of the same age, habits, and dispositions as themselves. After this the man should have the girl brought by means of her brother to some secure place and, having brought fire from the house of a Brahman, should proceed as before.

(4). The man should on the occasion of festivals get the daughter of the nurse to give the girl some intoxicating substance, and then cause her to be brought to some secure place under the pretense of some business, and there having enjoyed her before she recovers from her intoxication, should bring fire from the house of a Brahman, and proceed as before.

(5). The man should, with the connivance of the daughter of the nurse, carry off the girl from her house while she is asleep, and then, having enjoyed her before she recovers from her sleep, should bring fire from the house of a Brahman, and proceed as before.

(6). When the girl goes to a garden, or to some village in the neighborhood, the man should, with his friends, fall on her guards and, having killed them or frightened them away, forcibly carry her off, and proceed as before.

There are verses on this subject, as follows:

"In all the forms of marriage given in this chapter of this work, the one that precedes is better than the one that follows it, on account of its being more in accordance with the commands of religion, and therefore it is only when it is impossible to carry the former into practice that the latter should be resorted to. As the fruit of all good marriages is love, the Gandharva[3] form of marriage is respected, even though it is formed under unfavorable circumstances, because it fulfills the object sought for. Another cause of the respect accorded to the Gandharva form of marriage is that it brings forth happiness, causes less trouble in its performance than the other forms of marriage, and is above all the result of previous love.

---

[1] About this, see a story on the fatal effects of love at page 114 of *Early Ideas: a Group of Hindoo Stories*, collected and collated by Anaryan, W.H. Allen and Co., London, 1881.

[2] These forms of marriage differ from the four kinds of marriage mentioned in Chapter One, and are only to be made use of when the girl is gained over in the way mentioned in Chapters Three and Four.

[3] About the Gandharvavivaha form of marriage, see note to page 28 of Sir R.F. Burton's *Vickram and the Vampire: or, Tales of Hindu Devilry* (Longmans, Green & Co., London, 1870): "This form of matrimony was recognised by the ancient Hindus, and is frequent in books. It is a kind of Scottish wedding—ultra-Caledonian—taking place by mutual consent without any form or ceremony. The Gandharvas are heavenly minstrels of Indra's court, who are supposed to be witnesses."

Part Four

About a Wife

Chapter One

ON THE MANNER OF LIVING OF A VIRTUOUS WOMAN, AND OF HER BEHAVIOR DURING THE ABSENCE OF HER HUSBAND

A virtuous woman, who has affection for her husband, should act in conformity with his wishes as if he were a divine being, and with his consent should take upon herself the whole care of his family. She should keep the whole house well cleaned, and arrange flowers of various kinds in different parts of it, and make the floor smooth and polished so as to give the whole a neat and becoming appearance. She should surround the house with a garden, and place ready in it all the materials required for the morning, noon, and evening sacrifices. Moreover, she should herself revere the sanctuary of the household gods, for, says Gonardiya, "Nothing so much attracts the heart of a householder to his wife as a careful observance of the things mentioned above."

Toward the parents, relations, friends, sisters, and servants of her husband she should behave as they deserve. In the garden she should plant beds of green vegetables, bunches of the sugar cane, and clumps of the fig tree, the mustard plant, the parsley plant, the fennel plant, and the *Xanthochymus pictorius*. Clusters of various flowers, such as the *Trapa bispinosa*, the jasmine, the *Jasminum grandiflorum*, the yellow amaranth, the wild jasmine, the *Tabernaemontana coronaria*, the nadyawort, the Chinese rose, and others, should likewise be planted, together with the fragrant grass *Andropogon schaenanthus* and the fragrant root of the plant *Andropogon miricatus*. She should also have seats and arbors made in the garden, in the middle of which a well, tank, or pool should be dug.

The wife should always avoid the company of female beggars, female Buddhist mendicants, unchaste and roguish women, female fortunetellers and witches. As regards meals, she should always consider what her husband likes and dislikes, and what things are good for him, and what are injurious to him. When she hears the sound of his footsteps coming home she should at once get up, and be ready to do whatever he may command her, and either order her female servant to wash his feet, or wash them herself. When going anywhere with her husband she should put on her ornaments, and without his consent she should neither give nor accept invitations, or attend marriages and sacrifices, or sit in the company of female friends, or visit the temples of the Gods. And if she wants to engage in any kinds of games or sports, she should not do it against his will. In the same way she should always sit down after him, and get up before him, and should never awaken him when he is asleep. The kitchen should be situated in a quiet and retired place, so as not to be accessible to strangers, and should always look clean.

In the event of any misconduct on the part of her husband, she should not blame him excessively, though she be a little displeased. She should not use abusive language toward him, but rebuke him with conciliatory words, whether he be in the company of friends or alone. Moreover, she should not be a scold, for, says Gonardiya, "There is no cause of dislike on the part of a husband so great as this characteristic in a wife." Lastly, she should avoid bad expressions, sulky looks, speaking aside, standing in the doorway, and looking at passers-by, conversing in pleasure groves, and remaining in a lonely place for a long time; and finally she should always keep her body, her teeth, her hair, and everything belonging to her tidy, sweet, and clean.

When the wife wants to approach her husband in private, her dress should consist of many ornaments, various kinds of flowers, and a cloth decorated with different colors, and some sweet-smelling ointments or unguents. But her everyday dress should be composed of a thin, close-textured cloth, a few ornaments and flowers, and a little scent, not too much. She should also observe the fasts and vows of her husband, and when he tries to prevent her doing this, she should persuade him to let her do it.

At appropriate times of the year, and when they happen to be cheap, she should buy earth, bamboos, firewood, skins, and iron pots, as well as salt and oil. Fragrant substances, vessels made of the fruit of the plant *Wrightea antidysenterica*, or oval-leaved *Wrightea*, medicines, and other things which are always wanted, should be obtained when required and kept in a secret place of the house. The seeds of the radish, the potato, the common beet, the Indian wormwood, the mango, the cucumber, the eggplant, the kushmanda, the pumpkin gourd, the surana, the *Bignonia indica*, the sandalwood, the *Premna spinosa*, the garlic plant, the onion, and other vegetables, should be bought and sown at the proper seasons.

The wife, moreover, should not tell to strangers the amount of her wealth, or the secrets which her husband has confided to her. She should surpass all the women of her own rank in life in her cleverness, her appearance, her knowledge of cookery, her pride, and her manner of serving her husband. The expenditure of the year should be regulated by the profits. The milk that remains after the meals should be turned into ghee, or clarified butter. Oil and sugar should be prepared at home; spinning and weaving should also be done there; and a store of ropes and cords, and barks of trees for twisting into ropes, should be kept. She should also attend to the pounding and cleaning of rice, using its small grain and chaff in some way or other. She should pay the salaries of the servants, look after the tilling of the fields, the keeping of the flock and herds, superintend the making of vehicles, and take care of the rams, cocks, quails, parrots, starlings, cuckoos, peacocks, monkeys, and deer; and finally adjust the income and expenditure of the day. The worn-out clothes should be given to those servants who have done good work, in order to show them that their services have been appreciated, or they may be applied to some other use. The vessels in which wine is prepared, as well as those in which it is kept, should be carefully looked after, and put away at the proper time. All sales and purchases should also be well attended to. The friends of her husband she should welcome by presenting them with flowers, ointment, incense, betel leaves, and betel nut. Her father-in-law and mother-in-law she should treat as they deserve, always remaining dependent on their will, never contradicting them, speaking to them in few and not harsh words, not laughing loudly in their presence, and acting with their friends and enemies as with her own. In addition to the above she should not be vain, or too much taken up with her enjoyments. She should be liberal toward her servants, and reward them on holidays and festivals; and not give away anything without first making it known to her husband.

Thus ends discourse on the manner of a virtuous woman.

During the absence of her husband on a journey, the virtuous woman should wear only her auspicious ornaments, and observe the fasts in honor of the gods. While anxious to hear the news of her husband, she should still look after her household affairs. She should sleep near the elder women of the house, and make herself agreeable to them. She should look after and keep in repair the things that are liked by her husband, and continue the works that have been begun by him. To the abode of her relations she should not go except on occasions of joy and sorrow, and then she should go in her usual traveling dress, accompanied by her husband's servants, and not remain there for a long time. The fasts and feasts should be observed with the consent of the elders of the house. The resources should be increased by making purchases and sales according to the practice of the merchants, and by means of honest servants, superintended by herself. The income should be increased, and the expenditure diminished, as much as possible. And when her husband returns from his journey, she should receive him at first in her ordinary clothes, so that he may know in what way she has lived during his absence, and should bring to him some presents, as well as materials for the worship of the Deity.

Thus ends the part relating to the behavior of a wife during the absence of her husband on a journey.

There are also some verses on the subjects as follows:

"The wife, whether she be a woman of noble family or a virgin widow[1] remarried or a concubine, should lead a chaste life, devoted to her husband, and doing everything for his welfare. Women acting thus acquire Dharma, Artha, and Kama, obtain a high position, and generally keep their husbands devoted to them.

[1] This probably refers to a girl married in her infancy, or when very young, and whose husband had died before she arrived at the age of puberty. Infant marriages are still the common custom of the Hindus.

Chapter Two

ON THE CONDUCT OF THE ELDER WIFE TOWARD THE OTHER WIVES OF HER HUSBAND, AND ON THAT OF A YOUNGER WIFE TOWARD THE ELDER ONES; ON THE CONDUCT OF A VIRGIN WIDOW REMARRIED; OF A WIFE DISLIKED BY HER HUSBAND; OF THE WOMEN IN THE KING'S HAREM; AND, LASTLY, OF A HUSBAND TOWARD MANY WIVES

The causes of remarriage during the lifetime of the wife are as follows:

(1). The folly or ill temper of the wife.
(2). Her husband's dislike to her.
(3). The want of offspring.
(4). The continual birth of daughters.
(5). The incontinence of the husband.

From the very beginning a wife should endeavor to attract the heart of her husband by showing to him continually her devotion, her good temper, and her wisdom. If, however, she bears him no children, she should herself tell her husband to marry another woman. And when the second wife is married, and brought to the house, the first wife should give her a position superior to her own, and look upon her as a sister. In the morning the elder wife should forcibly make the younger one decorate herself in the presence of her husband, and should not mind all the husband's favor being given to her. If the younger wife does anything to displease her husband, the elder one should not neglect her, but should always be ready to give her most careful advice, and should teach her to do various things in the presence of her husband. Her children she should treat as her own, her attendants she should look upon with more regard even than on her own servants, her friends she should cherish with love and kindness, and her relatives with great honor.

When there are many other wives besides herself, the elder wife should associate with the one who is immediately next to her in rank and age, and should instigate the wife who has recently enjoyed her husband's favor to quarrel with the present favorite. After this, she should sympathize with the former and, having collected all the other wives together, should get them to denounce the favorite as a scheming and wicked woman, without, however, committing herself in any way. If the favorite wife happens to quarrel with the husband, then the elder wife should take her part and give her false encouragement, and thus cause the quarrel to be increased. If there be only a little quarrel between the two, the elder wife should do all she can to work it up into a large quarrel. But if after all this she finds that her husband still continues to love his favorite wife, she should then change her tactics, and endeavor to bring about a reconciliation between them, so as to avoid her husband's displeasure.

Thus ends discourse on the conduct of the elder wife.

The younger wife should regard the elder wife of her husband as her mother, and should not give anything away, even to her own relations, without her knowledge. She should tell her everything about herself, and not approach her husband without her permission. Whatever is told to her by the elder wife she should not reveal to others, and she should take care of the children of the senior even more than of her own. When alone with her husband she should serve him well, but should not tell him of the pain she suffers from the existence of a rival wife. She may also obtain from her husband some marks of his particular regard for her, and may tell him that she lives only for him and for the regard that he has for her. She should never reveal her love for her husband, or her husband's love for her to any person, either in pride or in anger, for a wife that reveals the secrets of her husband is despised by him. As for seeking to obtain the regard of her husband, Gonardiya says that it should always be done in private, for fear of the elder wife. If the elder wife be disliked by her husband, or be childless, she should sympathize with her, and should ask her husband to do the same, but should surpass her in leading the life of a chaste woman.

Thus ends discourse on the conduct of the younger wife towards the elder.

A widow in poor circumstances, or of a weak nature, who allies herself again to a man, is called a widow remarried.

The followers of Babhravya say that a virgin widow should not marry a person whom she may be obliged to leave because of his bad character, or of his being destitute of the excellent qualities of a man, or of his being obliged to have recourse to another person. Gonardiya is of the opinion that, as the cause of a widow's marrying again is her desire for happiness, and as happiness is secured by the possession of excellent qualities in her husband, joined to a love of enjoyment, it is therefore better to secure a person endowed with such qualities in the first instance. Vatsyayana, however, thinks that a widow may marry any person that she likes and that she thinks will suit her.

At the time of her marriage the widow should obtain from her husband the money to pay the cost of drinking parties, and picnics with her relations, and of giving them and her friends kindly gifts and presents; or she may do these things at her own cost if she likes. In the same way she may wear either her husband's ornaments or her own. As to the presents of affection mutually exchanged between the husband and herself, there is no fixed rule about them. If she leaves her husband after marriage of her own accord, she should restore to him whatever he may have given her, with the exception of the mutual presents. If, however, she is driven out of the house by her husband she should not return anything to him.

After her marriage she should live in the house of her husband like one of the chief members of the family, but should treat the other ladies of the family with kindness, the servants with generosity, and all the friends of the house with familiarity and good temper. She should show that she is better acquainted with the sixty-four arts than the other ladies of the house, and in any quarrels with her husband she should not rebuke him severely, but in private do everything that he wishes, and make use of the sixty-four ways of enjoyment. She should be obliging to the other wives of her husband; and to their children she should give presents, behave as their mistress, and make ornaments and playthings for their use. In the friends and servants of her husband she should confide more than in

his other wives, and finally she should have a liking for drinking parties, going to picnics, attending fairs and festivals, and for carrying out all kinds of games and amusements.

Thus ends discourse on the conduct of a virgin widow remarried.

A woman who is disliked by her husband, and annoyed and distressed by his other wives, should associate with the wife who is liked most by her husband and who serves him more than the others, and should teach her all the arts with which she is acquainted. She should act as the nurse of her husband's children and, having gained over his friends to her side, should through them make him acquainted of her devotion to him. She should be a leader in religious ceremonies and in vows and fasts, and should not hold too good an opinion of herself. When her husband is lying on his bed, she should go near him only when it is agreeable to him, and should never rebuke him, or show obstinacy in any way. If her husband happens to quarrel with any of his other wives, she should reconcile them to each other, and if he desires to see any woman secretly, she should manage to bring about the meeting between them. She should, moreover, make herself acquainted with the weak points of her husband's character, but always keep them secret, and on the whole behave herself in such a way as may lead him to look upon her as a good and devoted wife.

Here ends discourse on the conduct of a wife disliked by her husband.

The above sections will show how all the women of the king's seraglio are to behave, and therefore we shall now speak separately only about the king.

The female attendants in the harem (called severally Kanchukiyas,[1] Mahallarikas,[2] and Mahallikas[3]) should bring flowers, ointments, and clothes from the king's wives to the king; and he, having received these things, should give them as presents to the servants, along with the things worn by him the previous day. In the afternoon the king, having dressed and put on his ornaments, should interview the women of the harem, who should also be dressed and decorated with jewels. Then, having given to each of them such place and such respect as may suit the occasion and as they may deserve, he should carry on a cheerful conversation with them. After that, he should see such of his wives as may be virgin widows remarried, and after them the concubines and dancing girls. All these should be visited in their own private rooms.

When the king rises from his noonday sleep, the woman whose duty it is to inform the king regarding the wife who is to spend the night with him should come to him accompanied by the female attendants of that wife whose turn may have arrived in the regular course, and of her

who may have been accidentally passed over as her turn arrived, and of her who may have been unwell at the time of her turn. These attendants should place before the king the ointments and unguents sent by each of these wives, marked with the seal of her ring; and their names and their reasons for sending the ointments should be told to the king. After this the king accepts the ointment of one of them, who then is informed that her ointment has been accepted and that her day has been settled.[4]

At festivals, singing parties, and exhibitions all the wives of the king should be treated with respect and served with drinks.

But the women of the harem should not be allowed to go out alone, nor should any women outside the harem be allowed to enter except those whose character is well known. And, lastly, the work which the king's wives have to do should not be too fatiguing.

Thus ends discourse of the conduct of the king toward the women of the harem, and of their own conduct.

A man marrying many wives should act fairly toward them all. He should neither disregard nor pass over their faults, and should not reveal to one wife the love, passion, bodily blemishes, and confidential reproaches of the other. No opportunity should be given to any one of them of speaking to him about their rivals, and if one of them should begin to speak ill of another, he should chide her and tell her that she has exactly the same blemishes in her character. One of them he should please by secret confidence, another by secret respect, and another by secret flattery, and he should please them all by going to gardens, by amusements, by presents, by honoring their relations, by telling them secrets, and lastly by loving unions. A young woman who is of a good temper and who conducts herself according to the precepts of the Holy Writ (Dharma Shastras) wins her husband's attachment, and obtains a superiority over her rivals.

Thus ends discourse of the conduct of a husband toward many wives.

[1] A name given to the maidservants of the zenana of the king in ancient times, because they always kept their breasts covered with a cloth called Kanchuki. It was customary in the olden time for the maidservants to cover their breasts with a cloth, while the queens kept their breasts uncovered. This custom is distinctly to be seen in the Ajunta cave paintings.

[2] The meaning of this word is "superior woman," so it would seem that a Mahallarika must be a person in authority over the maidservants of the harem.

[3] This was also appertaining to the rank of women employed in the harem. In later times this place was given to eunuchs.

[4] As kings generally had many wives, it was usual for them to enjoy their wives by turns. But as it happened sometimes that some of them lost their turns owing to the king's absence, or to their being unwell, then in such cases the women whose turn had been passed over, and those whose turns had come, used to have a sort of lottery, and the ointment of all the claimants were sent to the king, who accepted the ointment of one of them, and thus settled the question.

Part Five

About the Wives of Other Men

Chapter One

ON THE CHARACTERISTICS OF MEN AND WOMEN, THE REASONS WHY WOMEN REJECT THE ADDRESSES OF MEN, MEN WHO HAVE SUCCESS WITH WOMEN, AND WOMEN WHO ARE EASILY GAINED OVER

The wives of other people may be resorted to on the occasions already described in Part One, Chapter Five, of this work, but the possibility of their acquisition, their fitness for cohabitation, the danger to oneself in uniting with them, and the future effect of these unions, should first of all be examined. A man may resort to the wife of another, for the purpose of saving his own life, when he perceives that his love for her proceeds from one degree of intensity to another. These degrees are ten in number, and are distinguished by the following marks:

(1). Love of the eye.
(2). Attachment of the mind.
(3). Constant reflection.
(4). Destruction of sleep.
(5). Emaciation of the body.
(6). Turning away from objects of enjoyment.
(7). Removal of shame.
(8). Madness.
(9). Fainting.
(10). Death.

Ancient authors say that a man should know the disposition, truthfulness, purity, and will of a young woman, as also the intensity or weakness of her passions from the form of her body, and from her characteristic marks and signs. But Vatsyayana is of the opinion that the forms of bodies and the characteristic marks or signs are but erring tests of character and that women should be judged by their conduct, by the outward expression of their thoughts, and by the movements of their bodies.

Now, as a general rule Gonikaputra says that a woman falls in love with every handsome man she sees, and so does every man at the sight of a beautiful woman, but frequently they do not take any further steps owing to various considerations. In love the following circumstances are peculiar to the woman. She loves without regard to right or wrong[1] and does not try to gain over a man simply for the attainment of some particular purpose. Moreover, when a man first makes up to her she naturally shrinks from him, even though she may be willing to unite herself with him. But when the attempts to gain her are repeated and renewed, she at last consents. But with a man, even though he may have begun to love, he conquers his feelings from a regard for morality and wisdom and, although his thoughts are often on the woman, he does not yield, even though an attempt be made to gain him over. He sometimes makes an attempt or effort to win the object of his affections and, having failed, he leaves her alone for the future. In the same way, once a woman is gained, he often becomes indifferent about her. As for the saying that a man does not care for what is easily gained, and desires only a thing which cannot be obtained without difficulty, it is only a matter of talk.

The causes of a woman rejecting the addresses of a man are as follows:
(1). Affection for her husband.
(2). Desire of lawful progeny.
(3). Want of opportunity.
(4). Anger at being addressed by the man too familiarly.
(5). Difference in rank of life.
(6). Want of certainty because of the man being devoted to traveling.

(7). Thinking that the man may be attached to some other person.
(8). Fear of the man's not keeping his intentions secret.
(9). Thinking that the man is too devoted to his friends, and has too great a regard for them.
(10). The apprehension that he is not in earnest.
(11). Bashfulness because of his being an illustrious man.
(12). Fear because of his being powerful, or possessed of too impetuous passion, in the case of the deer woman.
(13). Bashfulness because of his being too clever.
(14). The thought of having once lived with him on friendly terms only.
(15). Contempt of his want of knowledge of the world.
(16). Distrust of his low character.
(17). Disgust at his want of perception of her love for him.
(18). In the case of an elephant woman, the thought that he is a hare man, or a man of weak passion.
(19). Compassion lest any thing befall him because of his passion.
(20). Despair at her own imperfections.
(21). Fear of discovery.
(22). Disillusion at seeing his gray hair or shabby appearance.
(23). Fear that he may be employed by her husband to test her chastity.
(24). The thought that he has too much regard for morality.

Whichever of the above causes a man may detect, he should endeavor to remove it from the very beginning. Thus, the bashfulness that may arise from his greatness or his ability he should remove by showing his great love and affection for her. The difficulty of the want of opportunity, or of his inaccessibility, he should remove by showing her some easy way of access. The excessive respect entertained by the woman for him should be removed by making himself very familiar. The difficulties that arise from his being thought of low character he should remove by showing his valor and his wisdom; those that come from neglect by extra attention; and those that arise from fear by giving her proper encouragement.

The following are the men who generally obtain success with women:
(1). Men well versed in the science of love.
(2). Men skilled in telling stories.
(3). Men acquainted with women from their childhood.
(4). Men who have secured their confidence.
(5). Men who send presents to them.
(6). Men who talk well.
(7). Men who do things that they like.

(8). Men who have not loved other women previously.

(9). Men who act as messengers.

(10). Men who know their weak points.

(11). Men who are desired by good women.

(12). Men who are united with their female friends.

(13). Men who are good looking.

(14). Men who have been brought up with them.

(15). Men who are their neighbors.

(16). Men who are devoted to sexual pleasures, even though these be with their own servants.

(17). The lovers of the daughters of their nurse.

(18). Men who have been lately married.

(19). Men who like picnics and pleasure parties.

(20). Men who are liberal.

(21). Men who are celebrated for being very strong (bull men).

(22). Enterprising and brave men.

(23). Men who surpass their husbands in learning and good looks, in good qualities, and in liberality.

(24). Men whose dress and manner of living are magnificent.

The following are the women who are easily gained over:

(1). Women who stand at the door of their houses.

(2). Women who are always looking out on the street.

(3). Women who sit conversing in their neighbor's house.

(4). A woman who is always staring at you.

(5). A female messenger.

(6). A woman who looks sideways at you.

(7). A woman whose husband has taken another wife without any just cause.

(8). A woman who hates her husband, or who is hated by him.

(9). A woman who has nobody to look after her, or keep her in check.

(10). A woman who has not had any children.

(11). A woman whose family or caste is not well known.

(12). A woman whose children are dead.

(13). A woman who is very fond of society.

(14). A woman who is apparently very affectionate with her husband.

(15). The wife of an actor.

(16). A widow.

(17). A poor woman.

(18). A woman fond of enjoyments.

(19). The wife of a man with many younger brothers.

(20). A vain woman.

(21). A woman whose husband is inferior to her in rank or abilities.

(22). A woman who is proud of her skill in the arts.

(23). A woman disturbed in mind by the folly of her husband.

(24). A woman who has been married in her infancy to a rich man and, not liking him when she grows up, desires a man possessing a disposition, talents, and wisdom suitable to her own tastes.

(25). A woman who is slighted by her husband without any cause.

(26). A woman who is not respected by other women of the same rank or beauty as herself.

(27). A woman whose husband is devoted to traveling.

(28). The wife of a jeweler.

(29). A jealous woman.

(30). A covetous woman.

(31). An immoral woman.

(32). A barren woman.

(33). A lazy woman.

(34). A cowardly woman.

(35). A humpbacked woman.

(36). A dwarfish woman.

(37). A deformed woman.

(38). A vulgar woman.

(39). An ill-smelling woman.

(40). A sick woman.

(41). An old woman.

There are also two verses on the subject, as follows:

"Desire, which springs from nature, and which is increased by art, and from which all danger is taken away by wisdom, becomes firm and secure. A clever man, depending on his own ability, and observing carefully the ideas and thoughts of women, and removing the causes of their turning away from men, is generally successful with them."

Chapter Two

ON MAKING ACQUAINTANCE WITH THE WOMAN, AND ON EFFORTS TO GAIN HER OVER

Ancient authors are of the opinion that girls are not so easily seduced by employing female messengers as by the efforts of the man himself, but that the wives of others are more easily got at by the aid of female messengers than by the personal efforts of the man. But Vatsyayana lays it down that whenever it is possible a man should always act himself in these matters, and it is only when such is impracticable, or impossible, that female messengers should be employed. As for the saying that women who act and talk boldly and freely are to be won by the personal efforts of the man, and that women who do not possess those qualities are to be got at by female messengers, it is only a matter of talk.

Now, when a man himself acts in the matter, he should first of all make the acquaintance of the woman he loves in the following manner:

First, he should arrange to be seen by the woman, either on a natural or on a special opportunity. A natural opportunity is when one of them goes to the house of the other, and a special opportunity is when they meet either at the house of a friend, or a caste-fellow, or a minister, or a physician, as well as on the occasion of marriage, ceremonies, sacrifices, festivals, funerals, and garden parties.

Second, whenever they do meet, the man should be careful to look at her in such a way as to cause the state of his mind to be known to her; he should pull about his moustache, make a sound with his nails, cause his own ornaments to tinkle, bite his lower lip, and make various other signs of that description. When she is looking at him he should speak to his friends about her and other women, and should show to her his liberality and his appreciation of enjoyments. When sitting by the side of a female friend he should yawn and twist his body, contract his eyebrows, speak very slowly as if he were weary, and listen to her indifferently. A conversation having two meanings should

also be carried on with a child or some other person, apparently having regard to a third person, but really having reference to the woman he loves, and this way his love should be made manifest under the pretext of referring to others rather than to herself. He should make marks that have reference to her, on the earth with his nails, or with a stick, and should embrace and kiss a child in her presence, and give it the mixture of betel nut and betel leaves with his tongue, and press its chin with his fingers in a caressing way. All these things should be done at the proper time and in proper places.

Third, the man should fondle a child that may be sitting on her lap, and give it something to play with, and also take the same back again. Conversation with respect to the child may also be held with her, and in this manner he should gradually become well acquainted with her, and he should also make himself agreeable to her relations. Afterward, this acquaintance should be made a pretext for visiting her house frequently, and on such occasions he should converse on the subject of love in her absence, but within her hearing. As his intimacy with her increases, he should place in her charge some kind of deposit or trust, and take away from it a small portion at a time; or he may give her some fragrant substances, or betel nuts to be kept for him by her. After this, he should endeavor to make her well acquainted with his own wife, and get them to carry on confidential conversations, and to sit together in lonely places. In order to see her frequently he should arrange that the same goldsmith, the same jeweler, the same basket maker, the same dyer, and the same washerman be employed by the two families. And he should also pay her long visits openly under the pretense of being engaged with her on business, and one business should lead to another, so as to keep up the intercourse between them. Whenever she wants anything, or is in need of money, or wishes to acquire skill in one of the arts, he should cause her to understand that he is willing and able to do anything that she wants, to give her money, or teach her one of the arts, all these things being quite within his ability and power. In the same way he should hold discussions with her in company with other people, and they should talk of the doings and sayings of other persons, and examine different things like jewelry, precious stones, and so forth. On such occasions he should show her certain things with the values of which she may be unacquainted and, if she begins to dispute with him about the things or their value, he should not contradict her, but point out that he agrees with her in every way.

Thus ends discourse of the ways of making the aquaintance of the woman desired.

Now, after a girl has become acquainted with the man as above described, and has manifested her love to him by the various outward signs and by the motions of her body, the man should make every effort to gain her over. But as girls are not acquainted with sexual union, they should be treated with the greatest delicacy, and the man should proceed with considerable caution, though in the case of other women accustomed to sexual intercourse this is not necessary. When the intentions of the girl are known, and her bashfulness put aside, the man should begin to make use of her money, and an interchange of clothes, rings, and flowers should be made. In this, the man should take particular care that the things given by him are handsome and valuable. He should, moreover, receive from her a mixture of betel leaves, and when he is going to a party he should ask for the flower in her hair or the flower in her hand. If he himself gives her a flower, it should be a sweet-smelling one, marked with marks made by his nails or teeth. With increasing assiduity he should dispel her fears, and by degrees get her to go with him to some lonely place, and there he should embrace and kiss her. And finally, at the time of giving her some betel nut, or of receiving the same from her, or at the time of making an exchange of flowers, he should touch and press her private parts, thus bringing his efforts to a satisfactory conclusion.

When a man is endeavoring to seduce one woman, he should not attempt to seduce any other at the same time. But after he has succeeded with the first, and enjoyed her for a considerable time, he can keep her affections by giving her presents that she likes, and then commence making up to another woman. When a man sees the husband of a woman going to some place near his house, he should not enjoy the woman then, even though she may be easily gained over at the time. A wise man, having a regard for his reputation, should not think of seducing a woman who is apprehensive, timid, or not to be trusted, or one who is well guarded or possessed of a father-in-law or mother-in-law.

Chapter Three

EXAMINATION OF THE STATE OF A WOMAN'S MIND

When a man is trying to gain over a woman, he should examine the state of her mind, and act as follows:

If she listens to him, but does not manifest to him in any way her own intentions, he should then try to gain her over by means of a go-between.

If she meets him once, and again comes to meet him better dressed than before, or comes to him in some lonely place, he should be certain that she is capable of being enjoyed by the use of a little force. A woman who lets a man make up to her, but does not give herself up, even after a long time, should be considered a trifler in love; but owing to the fickleness of the human mind, even such a woman can be conquered by always keeping up a close acquaintance with her.

When a woman avoids the attentions of a man, and because of respect for him and pride in herself will not meet him or approach him, she can be gained over with difficulty, either by endeavoring to keep on familiar terms with her or else by an exceedingly clever go-between.

When a man makes up to a woman, and she reproaches him with harsh words, she should be abandoned at once.

When a woman reproaches a man, but at the same time acts affectionately toward him, she should be made love to in every way.

A woman who meets a man in lonely places, and puts up with the touch of his foot, but pretends, because of the indecision of her mind, not to be aware of it, should be conquered by patience, and by continued efforts as follows:

If she happens to go to sleep in his vicinity, he should put his left arm around her, and see when she awakens whether she repulses him in reality, or only as if she were desirous of the same thing being done to her again. And what is done by the arm can also be done by the foot. If the man succeeds in this point, he should embrace her more closely; and if she will not stand the embrace, and gets up, but behaves with him as usual the next day, he should consider then that she is not unwilling to be enjoyed by him. If, however, she does not appear again, the man should try to win her over by means of a go-between; and if, after having disappeared for some time she again appears, and behaves with him as usual, the man should then consider that she would not object to being united with him.

When a woman gives a man an opportunity, and makes her own love manifest to him, he should proceed to enjoy her. And the signs of a woman manifesting her love are these:

(1). She calls out to a man without being addressed by him in the first instance.

(2). She shows herself to him in secret places.

(3). She speaks to him tremblingly and inarticulately.

(4). The fingers of her hand and the toes of her feet are moistened with perspiration, and her face is blooming with delight.

(5). She occupies herself with shampooing his body and pressing his head.

(6). When shampooing him, she works with one hand only, and with the other she touches and embraces parts of his body.

(7). She remains with both hands placed on his body motionless, as if she had been surprised by something or was overcome by fatigue.

(8). She sometimes bends her face down upon his thighs, and when asked to shampoo them does not manifest any unwillingness to do so.

(9). She places one of her hands quite motionless on his body and, even though the man should press it between two members of his body, she does not remove it for a long time.

(10). Lastly, when she has resisted all the efforts of the man to gain her over, she returns to him the next day to shampoo his body as before.

When a woman neither gives encouragement to a man nor avoids him, but hides herself and remains in some lonely place, she must be got at by means of the female servant who may be near her. If when called by the man she acts in the same way, then she should be gained over by means of a skillful go-between. But if she will have nothing to say to the man, he should consider well before he begins any further attempts to gain her over.

Thus ends the examination of the state of a woman's mind.

A man should first get himself introduced to a woman, and then carry on a conversation with her. He should give her hints of his love for her and, if he finds from her replies that she receives these hints favorably, he should then set to work to gain her over without any fear. A woman who shows her love by outward signs to the man at his first interview should be gained over very easily. In the same way a lascivious woman, who when addressed in loving words replies openly in words expressive of her love, should be considered to have been gained over at that very moment. With regard to all women, whether they be wise, simple, or confiding, this rule is laid down that those who make an open manifestation of their love are easily gained over.

Chapter Four

ON THE BUSINESS OF A GO-BETWEEN

If a woman has manifested her love or desire either by signs or by motions of the body, and is afterward rarely or never seen anywhere, or if a woman is met for the first time, the man should get a go-between to approach her.

Now the go-between, having wheedled herself into the confidence of the woman by acting according to her disposition, should try to make her hate or despise her husband by holding artful conversations with her, by telling about medicines for getting children, by talking to her about other people, by tales of various kinds, by stories about the wives of other men, and by praising her beauty, wisdom, generosity, and good nature, and by saying to her, "It is indeed a pity that you, who are so excellent a woman in every way, should be possessed of a husband of this kind. Beautiful lady, he is not fit even to serve you." The go-between should further talk to the woman about the weakness of the passion of her husband, his jealousy, his roguery, his ingratitude, his aversion to enjoyments, his dullness, his meanness, and all the other faults that he may have, and with which she may be acquainted. She should particularly harp upon that fault or failing by which the wife may appear to be most affected. If the wife be a deer woman, and the husband a hare man, then there would be no fault in that direction, but in the event of his being a hare man, and she a mare woman or elephant woman, then this fault should be pointed out to her.

Gonikaputra is of the opinion that, when it is the first affair of the woman, or when her love has been only very secretly shown, the man should then secure and send to her a go-between with whom she may be already acquainted and in whom she confides.

But to return to our subject. The go-between should tell the woman about the obedience and love of the man and, as her confidence and affection increase, she should then explain to her the thing to be accomplished in the following way: "Hear this, O beautiful lady. This man, born of a good family, having seen you, has gone mad on your account. The poor young man, who is tender by nature, has never been distressed in such a way before, and it is highly probable that he will succumb under his present affliction, and experience the pains of death." If the woman listens with a favorable ear, then on the following day the go-between, having observed marks of good spirits in her face, in her eyes, and in her manner of conversation, should again converse with her on the subject of the man, and should tell her the stories of Ahalya[1] and Indra, of Shakuntala[2] and Dushyanti, and such others as may be fit for the occasion. She should also describe to her the strength of the man, his talents, his skill in the sixty-four sorts of enjoyments mentioned by Babhravya, his good looks, and his liaison with some praiseworthy woman, no matter whether this last ever took place or not.

In addition to this, the go-between should carefully note the behavior of the woman, which if favorable would be as follows: She would address her with a smiling look, would seat herself close beside her, and ask her, "Where have you been? What have you been doing? Where did you dine? Where did you sleep? Where have you been sitting?" Moreover, the woman would meet the go-between in lonely places and tell her stories there, would yawn contemplatively, draw long sighs, give her presents, remember her on occasions of festivities, dismiss her with a wish to see her again, and say to her jestingly, "O well-speaking woman, why do you speak these bad words to me?" She would discourse on the sin of her union with the man, would not tell her about any previous visits or conversations that she may have had with him, but would wish to be asked about these, and lastly would laugh at the man's desire, but would not reproach him in any way.

Thus ends the behavior of the woman with the go-between.

47

When the woman manifests her love in the manner above described, the go-between should increase it by bringing to her love tokens from the man. But if the woman be not acquainted with the man personally, the go-between should win her over by extolling and praising his good qualities, and by telling stories about his love for her. Here Auddalaka says that, when a man and woman are not personally acquainted with each other, and have not shown each other any signs of affection, the employment of a go-between is useless.

The followers of Babhravya, on the other hand, affirm that even though they be personally unacquainted, but have shown each other signs of affection, there is an occasion for the employment of a go-between. Gonikaputra asserts that a go-between should be employed, provided they are acquainted with each other, even though no signs of affection may have passed between them. Vatsyayana, however, lays it down that even though they may not be personally acquainted with each other, and may not have shown each other any signs of affection, still they are both capable of placing confidence in a go-between.

Now the go-between should show to the woman the presents, such as the betel nut and the betel leaves, the perfumes, the flowers, and the rings the man may have given to her for the sake of the woman, and on these presents should be impressed the marks of the man's teeth and nails, and other signs. On the cloth that he may send he should draw with saffron both his hands joined together as if in earnest entreaty.

The go-between should also show to the woman ornamental figures of various kinds cut in leaves, together with ear ornaments, and chaplets made of flowers containing love letters expressive of the desire of the man,[3] and she should cause her to send affectionate presents to the man in return. After they have mutually accepted each other's presents, a meeting should be arranged between them on the faith of the go-between.

The followers of Babhravya say that this meeting should take place at the time of going to the temple of a deity; or on occasions of fairs, garden parties, theatrical performances, marriages, sacrifices, festivals, and funerals, as well as at the time of going to the river to bathe, or at times of natural calamities,[4] during fear of robbers or of hostile invasions of the country.

Gonikaputra is of the opinion, however, that these meetings had better be brought about in the abodes of female friends, mendicants, astrologers, and ascetics. But Vatsyayana decides that only that place is well suited for the purpose which has proper means of ingress and egress, and where arrangements have been made to prevent any accidental occurrence, and where a man who has once entered the house can also leave it at the proper time without any disagreeable encounter.

Now, go-betweens or female messengers are of the following different kinds:

(1). A go-between who takes upon herself the whole burden of the business.

(2). A go-between who does only a limited part of the business.

(3). A go-between who is the bearer of a letter only.

(4). A go-between acting on her own account.

(5). The go-between of an innocent young woman.

(6). A wife serving as a go-between.

(7). A mute go-between.

(8). A go-between who acts the part of the wind.

(1). A woman who, having observed the mutual passion of a man and woman, brings them together and arranges it by the power of her own intellect, such a one is called a go-between who takes upon herself the whole burden of the business. This kind of go-between is chiefly employed when the man and the woman are already acquainted with each other, and have conversed together, and in such cases she is sent not only by the man (as is always done in all other cases), but by the woman also. The above name is also given to a go-between who, perceiving that the man and the woman are suited to each other, tries to bring about a union between them even though they are not acquainted with each other.

(2). A go-between who, perceiving that some part of the affair is already done, or that the advances on the part of the man are already made, completes the rest of the business is called a go-between who performs only a limited part of the business.

(3). A go-between who simply carries messages between a man and a woman who love each other but who cannot frequently meet is called the bearer of a letter or message.

This name is also given to one who is sent by either of the lovers to acquaint either the one or the other with the time and place of their meeting.

(4). A woman who goes herself to a man, and tells him of her having enjoyed sexual union with him in a dream, and expresses her anger at his wife having rebuked him for calling her by the name of her rival instead of by her own name, and gives him something bearing the marks of her teeth and nails, and informs him that she knew she was formerly desired by him, and asks him privately whether she or his wife is the better looking, such a person is called a woman who is a go-between for herself. Now, such a woman should be met and interviewed by the man in private and secretly.

The above name is also given to a woman who, having made an agreement with some other woman to act as her

go-between, gains the man for herself by making him personally acquainted with herself, and thus causes the other woman to fail. The same applies to a man who, acting as a go-between for another, and having no previous connection with the woman, gains her for himself, and thus causes the failure of the other man.

(5). A young woman who has gained the confidence of the innocent young wife of any man, and who has learned her secrets without exercising any pressure on her mind, and found out from her how her husband behaves to her, if this woman then teaches her the art of securing his favor, and decorates her so as to show her love, and instructs her how and when to be angry, or to pretend to be so, and then, having herself made marks of the nails and teeth on the body of the wife, gets the latter to send for her husband to show these marks to him, and thus excite him for enjoyment, such is called the go-between of an innocent young woman. In such cases the man should send replies to his wife through the same woman.

(6). When a man gets his wife to gain the confidence of a woman whom he wants to enjoy, and to call on her and talk to her about the wisdom and ability of her husband, that wife is called a wife serving as a go-between. In this case the feelings of the woman with regard to the man should also be made known through the wife.

(7). When any man sends a girl or a female servant to any woman under some pretext or other, and places a letter in her bouquet of flowers, or in her ear ornaments, or marks something about her with his teeth or nails, that girl or female servant is called a mute go-between. In this

case the man should expect an answer from the woman through the same person.

(8). A person who carries a message to a woman which has a double meaning, or which relates to some past transactions, or which is unintelligible to other people, is called a go-between who acts the part of the wind. In this case the reply should be asked for through the same woman.

Thus ends discourse of the different kinds of go-betweens.

A female astrologer, a female servant, a female beggar, or a female artist are well acquainted with the business of a go-between, and very soon gain the confidence of other women. Any one of them can raise enmity between any two persons if she wishes to do so, or extol the loveliness of any woman that she wishes to praise, or describe the arts practiced by other women in sexual union. They can also speak highly of the love of a man, of his skill in sexual enjoyment, and of the desire of other women, more beautiful even than the woman they are addressing, for him, and explain the restraint under which he may be at home.

Lastly, a go-between can by the artfulness of her conversation unite a woman with a man, even though he may not have been thought of by her, or though she may have been considered beyond his aspirations. She can also bring back a man to a woman who, owing to some cause or other, has separated himself from her.

[1] The wife of the sage Gautama; she was seduced by Indra the king of the gods.

[2] The heroine of one of the best, if not the best, of Hindu plays, and the best known in Sanscrit dramatic literature. It was first brought to notice by Sir William Jones, and has been well and poetically translated by Dr. Monier William under the title of Sakoontala or the lost ring, an Indian drama, translated into English prose and verse from the Sanscrit by Kalidasa.

[3] It is presumed that something like the following French verses are intended:
Quand on a juré le plus profond hommage,
Voulez-vous qu'infidèle on change de langage;
Vous seul captivez mon esprit et mon coeur
Que je puisse dans vos bras seuls gouter le bonheur;
Je voudrais, mais en vain, que mon coeur en délire
Couche où ce papier n'oserait vous dire.
Avec soin, de ces vers lisez leurs premiers mots,
Vous verrez quel remède il faut à tous mes maux.

(NBM rough translation:
When one has sworn the deepest homage,
Would one, unfaithful, want to change language;
You alone my heart and spirit captivate
That I may only in your arms know of happiness profligate;
I wish, unrequited, my heart
May lie where this paper dare not impart.
With care you must read what the first few verses express
So that you may see the cure for my distress.)
    Or these:
Quand on vous voit, on vous aime;
Quand on vous aime, où vous voit-on?
    (NBM rough translation:
When one sees you, one loves you;
When one loves you, where are you to be seen?)

[4] It is supposed that storms, earthquakes, famines and pestilent diseases are here alluded to.

Chapter Five

ON THE LOVE OF PERSONS IN AUTHORITY FOR THE WIVES OF OTHER MEN

Kings and their ministers have no access to the abodes of others; moreover, their mode of living is constantly watched and observed and imitated by the people at large, just as the animal world, seeing the sun rise, get up after him, and when he sets in the evening, lie down again in the same way. Therefore persons in authority should not do any improper act in public, since such are reprehensible for one in their position, and would be deserving of censure. But if they find that such an act is necessary to be done, they should make use of the proper means, as described in the following paragraphs.

The head man of the village (Gramani), the king's officer employed there, and the man[1] whose business it is to glean corn, can gain over female villagers simply by asking them. It is on this account that this class of woman are called unchaste women by voluptuaries.

The union of the above-mentioned men with this class of woman takes place on the occasions of unpaid labor, of filling the granaries in their houses, of taking things in and out of the house, of cleaning the houses, of working in the fields, and of purchasing cotton, wool, flax, hemp, and thread, and at the season of the purchase, sale, and exchange of various other articles, as well as at the time of doing various other works. In the same way the superintendents of cow pens enjoy the women in the cow pens; and officers who have the superintendence of widows, of women who are without supporters, and of women who have left their husbands have sexual intercourse with these women. The intelligent accomplish their object by wandering at night in the village, while villages also unite with the wives of their sons, being much alone with them. Lastly, the superintendents of markets have a great deal to do with female villagers at the time of their making purchases in the market.

(1). During the festival of the eighth moon, that is, during the bright half of the month of Nargashirsha, as also during the moonlight festival of the month of Kartika, and the spring festival of Chaitra, the women of cities and towns generally visit the king's harem in the royal palace. These visitors go to the several apartments of the women of the harem, as they are acquainted with them, and pass the night in conversation, and in proper sports and amusement, and go away in the morning. On such occasions a female attendant of the king (previously acquainted with the woman whom the king desires), should loiter about, and accost this woman when she sets out to go home, and induce her to come and see the amusing things in the palace. Even before these festivals, the attendant should have caused it to be intimated to this woman that on the occasion of this festival she would show her all the interesting things in the royal palace. Accordingly she should show her the bower of the coral creeper, the garden house with its floor inlaid with precious stones, the bower of grapes, the building on the water, the secret passages in the walls of the palace, the pictures, the sporting animals, the machines, the birds, and the cages of the lions and the tigers. After this, when alone with her, she should tell her about the love of the king for her, and should describe to her the good fortune which would attend upon her union with the king, giving her at the time a strict promise of secrecy. If the woman does not accept the offer, the attendant should conciliate and please her with handsome presents befitting the position of the king, and having accompanied her for some distance should dismiss her with great affection.

(2). Or, having made the acquaintance of the husband of the woman whom the king desires, the wives of the king should get the wife to pay them a visit in the harem, and on this occasion a female attendant of the king, having been sent thither, should act as described above.

(3). Or one of the king's wives should get acquainted with the woman that the king desires, by sending one of the female attendants to her, who should, on their becoming more intimate, induce her to come and see the royal abode. Afterward, when she has visited the harem, and acquired confidence, a female confidant of the king, sent thither, should act as before described.

(4). Or the king's wife should invite the woman whom the king desires, to come to the royal palace, so that she might see the practice of the art in which the king's wife may be skilled and, after she has come to the harem, a female attendant of the king, sent thither, should act as before described.

(5). Or a female beggar, in league with the king's wife, should say to the woman desired by the king, and whose husband may have lost his wealth, or may have some cause for fear from the king, "This wife of the king has influence over him; she is, moreover, naturally kindhearted, and we must therefore go to her in this matter. I shall arrange for your entrance into the harem, and she will do away with all cause of danger and fear from the king." If the woman accepts this offer, the female beggar should take her two or three times to the harem, and the king's wife there should give her a promise of protection. After this, when the woman, delighted with her reception and promise of protection, again goes to the harem, then a female attendant of the king, sent thither, should act as directed.

(6). What has been said above regarding the wife of one who has some cause for fear from the king applies also to the wives of those who seek service under the king or who are oppressed by the king's ministers, or who are poor, or who are not satisfied with their position, or who are desirous of gaining the king's favor, or who wish to become famous among the people, or who are oppressed by the members of their own caste or who want to injure their caste fellows, or who are spies of the king, or who have any other object to attain.

(7). Lastly, if the woman desired by the king be living with some person who is not her husband, then the king should cause her to be arrested and, having made her a slave because of her crime, should place her in the harem. Or the king should cause his ambassador to quarrel with the husband of the woman desired by him, and should then imprison her as the wife of an enemy of the king, and by this means should place her in the harem.

Thus ends discourse of the means of gaining over the wives of others secretly.

The above-mentioned ways of gaining over the wives of other men are chiefly practiced in the palaces of the kings. But a king should never enter the abode of another person, for Abhira[2] the King of the Kottas was killed by a washerman while in the house of another, and in the same way Jayasana the King of the Kashis was slain by the commandant of his Cavalry (Senapati).

But according to the customs of some countries, there are facilities for kings to make love to the wives of other men. Thus in the country of the Andras,[3] the newly married daughters of the people thereof enter the king's harem with some presents on the tenth day of their marriage, and having been enjoyed by the king are then dismissed. In the country of the Vatsagulmas,[4] the wives of the chief ministers approach the king at night to serve him. In the country of the Vaidarbhas,[5] the beautiful wives of the inhabitants pass a month in the king's harem under the pretense of affection for the king. In the country of the Aparatakas,[6] the people gave their beautiful wives as presents to the ministers and the kings. And lastly in the country of the Saurashtras,[7] the women of the city and the country enter the royal harem for the king's pleasure, either together or separately.

There are also two verses on the subject, as follows:

"The above and other ways are the means employed in different countries by kings with regards to the wives of other persons. But a king who has the welfare of his people at heart should not on any account put them into practice."

"A king who has conquered the six[8] enemies of mankind becomes the master of the whole earth."

---

[1] This is a phrase used for the man who does the work of everybody, and who is fed by the whole village.

[2] The exact date of the reign of these kings is not known. It is supposed to have been about the beginning of the Christian era.

[3] The modern country of Tailangam, which is to the south of Rajamundry.

[4] Supposed to be a tract of the country to the south of Malwa.

[5] Now known by the name of Berar. Its capital was Kundinpura, which has been identified with the modern Oomravati.

[6] Also called Aparantakas, being the northern and southern Concan.

[7] The modern province of Katteeawar. Its capital was called Girinaguda, or the modern Junagurh.

[8] These are Lust, Anger, Avarice, Spiritual Ignorance, Pride, and Envy.

Chapter Six

ABOUT THE WOMEN OF THE ROYAL HAREM, AND ON THE KEEPING OF ONE'S OWN WIFE

The women of the royal harem cannot see or meet any men on account of their being strictly guarded; neither do they have their desires satisfied, because their only husband is common to many wives. For this reason, among themselves they give pleasure to each other in various ways as now described.

Having dressed the daughters of their nurses, or their female friends, or their female attendants, like men, they accomplish their object by means of bulbs, roots, and fruits having the form of the lingam, or they lie down upon the statue of a male figure, in which the lingam is visible and erect.

Some kings, who are compassionate, take or apply certain medicines to enable them to enjoy many wives in one night, simply for the purpose of satisfying the desire of their women, though they perhaps have no desire of their own. Others enjoy with great affection only those wives that they particularly like, while others take them only as the turn of each wife arrives, in due course. Such are the ways of enjoyment prevalent in Eastern countries, and what is said about the means of enjoyment of the female is also applicable to the male.

By means of their female attendants, the ladies of the royal harem generally get men into their apartments in the disguise or dress of women. Their female attendants, and the daughters of their nurses, who are acquainted with their secrets, should exert themselves to get men to come to the harem in this way by telling them of the good fortune attending it, and by describing the facilities of entering and leaving the palace, the large size of the premises, the carelessness of the sentinels, and the irregularities of the attendants about the persons of the royal wives. But these women should never induce a man to enter the harem by telling him falsehoods, for that would probably lead to his destruction.

As for the man himself, he had better not enter a royal harem, even though it may be easily accessible, because of the numerous disasters to which he may be exposed there. If, however, he wants to enter it, he should first ascertain whether there is an easy way to get out, whether it is closely surrounded by the pleasure garden, whether it has separate enclosures belonging to it, whether the sentinels are careless, whether the king has gone abroad, and then, when he is called by the women of the harem, he should carefully observe the localities, and enter by the way pointed out by them. If he is able to manage it, he should hang about the harem every day, and, under some pretext or other, make friends with the sentinels, and show himself attached to the female attendants of the harem, who may have become acquainted with his design, and to whom he should express his regret at not being able to obtain the object of his desire. Lastly, he should cause the whole business of a go-between to be done by the woman who may have access to the harem, and he should be careful to be able to recognize the emissaries of the king.

When a go-between has no access to the harem, then the man should stand in some place where the lady whom he loves and whom he is anxious to enjoy can be seen.

If that place is occupied by the king's sentinels, he should then disguise himself as a female attendant of the lady who comes to the place, or passes by it. When she looks at him he should let her know his feeling by outward signs and gestures, and should show her pictures, things with double meanings, chaplets of flowers, and rings. He should carefully mark the answer she gives, whether by word or by sign or by gesture, and should then try and get into the harem. If he is certain of her coming to some particular place, he should conceal himself there, and at the appointed time should enter along with her as one of the guards. He may also go in and out, concealed in a folded bed, or bed covering, or with his body made invisible,[1] by means of external applications, a recipe for one of which is as follows:

The heart of an ichneumon, the fruit of the long gourd (Tumbaki), and the eyes of a serpent should all be burned without letting out the smoke; the ashes should then be ground and mixed in equal quantities with water. By putting this mixture upon the eyes a man can go about unseen.

Other means of invisibility are prescribed by Dhyana Brahmans and Yogashiras.

Again, the man may enter the harem during the festival of the eighth moon in the month of Nargashirsha, and during the moonlight festivals when the female attendants of the harem are all busily occupied, or in confusion.

The following principles are laid down on this subject.

The entrance of young men into harems, and their exit from them, generally take place when things are being brought into the palace, or when things are being taken out of it, or when drinking festivals are going on, or when the female attendants are in a hurry, or when the residence of some of the royal ladies is being changed, or when the king's wives go to gardens, or to fairs, or when they enter the palace on their return from them, or lastly, when the king is absent on a long pilgrimage. The women of the royal harem know each other's secrets and, having but one object to attain, they give assistance to each other. A young man who enjoys all of them, and who is common to them all, can continue enjoying his union with them so long as it is kept quiet and is not known abroad.

Now, in the country of the Aparatakas the royal ladies are not well protected, and consequently many young men are passed into the harem by the women who have access to the royal palace. The wives of the king of the Abhira country accomplish their objects with those sentinels in the harem who bear the name of Kshatriyas. The royal ladies in the country of the Vatsagulmas cause such men as are suitable to enter into the harem along with their female messengers. In the country of the Vaidarbhas the sons of the royal ladies enter the royal harem when they please, and enjoy the women, with the exception of their own mothers. In the Stri Rajya the wives of the king are enjoyed by his caste fellows and relations. In the Gandak country the royal wives are enjoyed by Brahmans, friends, servants, and slaves. In the Samdhava country, servants, foster children, and other persons like them enjoy the women of the harem. In the country of the Himalayas adventurous citizens bribe the sentinels and the harem. In the country of the Vanyas and the Kalmyas, Brahmans, with the knowledge of the king, enter the harem under the pretense of giving flowers to the ladies, and speak with them from behind a curtain, and from such conversation union afterward takes place. Lastly, the women in the harem of the king of the Prachyas conceal one young man in the harem for every batch of nine or ten women.

Thus act the wives of the others.

For these reasons a man should guard his own wife. Old authors say that a king should select for sentinels in his harem such men as have had their freedom from carnal desire well tested. But such men, though free themselves from carnal desire, by reason of their fear or avarice may cause other persons to enter the harem, and therefore Gonikaputra says that kings should place such men in the harem as may have had their freedom from carnal desires, their fears, and their avarice well tested. Lastly, Vatsyayana says that under the influence of Dharma[2] people might be admitted, and therefore men should be selected who are free from carnal desires, fear, avarice, and Dharma.[3]

The followers of Babhravya say that a man should cause his wife to associate with a young woman who would tell him the secrets of other people, and thus find out from her about his wife's chastity. But Vatsyayana says that, as wicked persons are always successful with women, a man should not cause his innocent wife to be corrupted by bringing her into the company of a deceitful woman.

The following are the causes of the destruction of a woman's chastity:
Always going into society, and sitting in company
Absence of restraint
The loose habits of her husband
Want of caution in her relations with other men
Continued and long absence of her husband
Living in a foreign country
Destruction of her love and feelings by her husband
The company of loose women
The jealousy of her husband

There are also the following verses on the subject:
"A clever man, learning from the Shastras the ways of winning over the wives of other people, is never deceived in the case of his own wives. No one, however, should make use of these ways for seducing the wives of others, because they do not always succeed, and, moreover, often cause disasters, and the destruction of Dharma and Artha. This book, which is intended for the good of the people, and to teach them the ways of guarding their own wives, should not be made use of merely for gaining over the wives of others."

[1] The way to make oneself invisible; the knowledge of the art of transmigration, or changing ourselves or others into any shape or form by the use of charms and spells; the power of being in two places at once; and other occult sciences are frequently referred to in Oriental literature.

[2] This may be considered as meaning religious influence, and alludes to persons who might be gained over by that means.

[3] It will be noted from the above remarks that eunuchs do not appear to have been employed in the king's harem in those days, though they seem to have been employed for other purposes. See Part II, Chapter XI.

Part Six

About Courtesans

INTRODUCTORY REMARKS

This Part VI, about courtesans, was prepared by Vatsyayana from a treatise on the subject that was written by Dattaka for the women of Pataliputra (the modern Patna) some two thousand years ago. Dattaka's work does not appear to be extant now, but this abridgement of it is very clever, and quite equal to any of the productions of Emile Zola and other writers of the realistic school of today.

Although a great deal has been written on the subject of the courtesan, nowhere will be found a better description of her, of her belonging, of her ideas, and of the working of her mind, than is contained in the following pages.

The details of the domestic and social life of the early Hindus would not be complete without mention of the courtesan, and Part VI is entirely devoted to this subject. The Hindus have ever had the good sense to recognize courtesans as a part and portion of human society and, so long as they behaved themselves with decency and propriety, they were regarded with a certain respect. Anyhow, they have never been treated in the East with that brutality and contempt so common in the West, while their education has always been of a kind superior to that bestowed upon the rest of womankind in Oriental countries.

In the earlier days the well-educated Hindu dancing girl and courtesan doubtless resembled the Hetera of the Greeks and, being educated and amusing, were far more acceptable as companions than the generality of the married or unmarried women of that period. At all times and in all countries, there has ever been a little rivalry between the chaste and the unchaste. But while some women are born courtesans, and follow the instincts of their nature in every class of society, it has been truly said by some authors that every woman has got an inkling of the profession in her nature, and does her best, as a general rule, to make herself agreeable to the male sex.

The subtlety of women, their wonderful perceptive powers, their knowledge, and their intuitive appreciation of men and things, are all shown in the following pages, which may be looked upon as a concentrated essence that has been since worked up into detail by many writers in every quarter of the globe.

Chapter One

ON THE CAUSES OF A COURTESAN RESORTING TO MEN, ON THE MEANS OF ATTACHING TO HERSELF THE MAN DESIRED, AND ON THE KIND OF MAN THAT IT IS DESIRED TO BE ACQUAINTED WITH

By having intercourse with men, courtesans obtain sexual pleasure, as well as their own maintenance. Now when a courtesan takes up with a man from love, the action is natural; but when she resorts to him for the purpose of getting money, her action is artificial or forced. Even in this latter case, however, she should conduct herself as if her love were indeed natural, because men repose their confidence on those women who apparently love them. In making known her love to the man, she should show an entire freedom from avarice, and for the sake of her future credit she should abstain from acquiring money from him by unlawful means.

A courtesan, well dressed and wearing her ornaments, should sit or stand at the door of her house and, without exposing herself too much, should look on the public road so as to be seen by the passersby, she being like an object on view for sale.[1] She should form friendships with such persons as would enable her to separate men from other women, and attach them to herself, to repair her own misfortunes, to acquire wealth, and to protect her from being bullied, or set upon by persons with whom she may have dealings of some kind or another.

These persons are:
The guards of the town, or the police
The officers of the courts of justice
Astrologers
Powerful men, or men with interests
Learned men
Teachers of the sixty-four arts
Pithamardas or confidants
Vitas or parasites
Vidushakas or jesters
Flower sellers
Perfumers
Vendors of spirits
Washermen
Barbers
Beggars
And such other persons as may be found necessary for the particular object to be acquired.

The following kinds of men may be taken up with, simply for the purpose of getting their money:
Men of independent income
Young men
Men who are free from any ties
Men who hold places of authority under the king
Men who have secured their means of livelihood without difficulty.
Men possessed of unfailing sources of income
Men who consider themselves handsome
Men who are always praising themselves
One who is a eunuch, but wishes to be thought a man
One who hates his equals
One who is naturally liberal
One who has influence with the king or his ministers
One who is always fortunate
One who is proud of his wealth
One who disobeys the orders of his elders
One upon whom the members of his caste keep an eye
An only son whose father is wealthy
An ascetic who is internally troubled with desire
A brave man
A physician of the king
Previous acquaintances

On the other hand, those who are possessed of excellent qualities are also to be resorted to for the sake of love and fame. Such men are as follows:
Men of high birth, learned, with a good knowledge of the world, and doing the proper things at the proper times; poets, good storytellers, eloquent men, energetic men

skilled in various arts, farseeing into the future, possessed of great minds, full of perseverence, of a firm devotion, free from anger, liberal, affectionate to their parents, and with a liking for all social gatherings, skilled in completing verses begun by others and in various other sports, free from all disease, possessed of a perfect body, strong, and not addicted to drinking, powerful in sexual enjoyment, sociable, showing love toward women and attracting their hearts to himself but not entirely devoted to them, possessed of independent means of livelihood, free from envy and, last of all, free from suspicion.

Such are the good qualities of a man.

The woman also should have the following characteristics:

She should be possessed of beauty and amiability, with auspicious body marks. She should have a liking for good qualities in other people, as well as a liking for wealth. She should take delight in sexual unions resulting from love, and should be of firm mind, and of the same class as the man with regard to sexual enjoyment.

She should always be anxious to acquire and obtain experience and knowledge, be free from avarice, and always have a liking for social gatherings, and for the arts.

The following are the ordinary qualities of all women:

To be possessed of intelligence, good disposition, and good manners; to be straightforward in behavior, and to be grateful; to consider well the future before doing anything; to possess activity, to be of consistent behavior, and to have a knowledge of the proper times and places for doing things; to speak always without meanness, loud laughter, malignity, anger, avarice, dullness, or stupidity, to have a knowledge of the Kama Sutra, and to be skilled in all the arts connected with it.

The faults of the women are to be known by the absence of any of the above-mentioned good qualities.

The following kinds of men are not fit to be resorted to by courtesans:

One who is consumptive, one who is sickly, one whose mouth contains worms, one whose breath smells like human excrement, one whose wife is dear to him, one who speaks harshly, one who is always suspicious, one who is avaricious, one who is pitiless, one who is a thief, one who is self-conceited, one who has a liking for sorcery, one who does not care for respect or disrespect, one who can be gained over even by his enemies by means of money, and lastly, one who is extremely bashful.

Ancient authors are of the opinion that the causes of a courtesan resorting to men are: love, fear, money, pleasure, returning some act of enmity, curiosity, sorrow, constant intercourse, Dharma, celebrity, compassion, the desire of having a friend, shame, the likeness of the man to some beloved person, the search after good fortune, getting rid of the love of somebody else, being of the same class as the man with respect to sexual union, living in the same place, constancy, and poverty. But Vatsyayana decides that desire of wealth, freedom from misfortune, and love are the only causes that affect the union of courtesans with men.

Now, a courtesan should not sacrifice money to her love, because money is the chief thing to be attended to. But in cases of fear, and so on, she should pay regard to strength and other qualities. Moreover, even though she be invited by any man to join him, she should not at once consent to a union, because men are apt to despise things which are easily acquired. On such occasions she should first send the shampooers and the singers and the jesters who may be in her service, or in their absence the Pithamadras, or confidants, and others, to find out the state of his feelings and the condition of his mind. By means of these persons she should ascertain whether the man is pure or impure, affected or unaffected, capable of attachment, or indifferent, liberal or niggardly; and if she finds him to her liking, she should then employ the Vita and others to attach his mind to her.

Accordingly, the Pithamarda should bring the man to her house, under the pretense of seeing the fights of quails, cocks, and rams, of hearing the mynah (a kind of starling) talk, or of seeing some other spectacle, or the practice of some art; or he may take the woman to the abode of the man. After this, when the man comes to her house, the woman should give him something capable of producing curiosity and love in his heart, such as an affectionate present, telling him that it was specially designed for his use. She should also amuse him for a long time by telling him such stories and doing such things as he may take most delight in. When he goes away she should frequently send to him a female attendant, skilled in carrying on a jesting conversation, and also a small present at the same time. She should also sometimes go to him herself under the pretense of some business, and accompanied by the Pithamarda.

Thus ends discourse of the means of attaching to herself the man desired.

There are also some verses on the subject, as follows:
"When a lover comes to her abode, a courtesan should give him a mixture of betel leaves and betel nut, garlands of flowers, and perfumed ointments, and, showing her skill in arts, should entertain him with a long conversation. She should also give him some loving presents, and make an exchange of her own things with him, and at the same time

should show him her skill in sexual enjoyment. When a courtesan is thus united with her lover, she should always delight him by affectionate gifts, by conversation, and by the application of tender means of enjoyment."

¹ In England the lower classes of courtesans walk the streets; in India and other places in the East, they all sit at the windows, or at the doors of their houses.

Chapter Two

ON LIVING LIKE A WIFE

When a courtesan is living as a wife with her lover, she should behave like a chaste woman, and do everything to his satisfaction. Her duty in this respect, in short, is that she should give him pleasure, but should not become attached to him, though behaving as if she were really attached.

Now the following is the manner in which she is to conduct herself, so as to accomplish the above-mentioned purpose. She should have a mother dependent on her, one who should be represented as very harsh, and who looked upon money as her chief object in life. In the event of there being no mother, then an old and confidential nurse should play the same role. The mother or nurse, on her part, should appear to be displeased with the lover, and forcibly take her away from him. The woman herself should always show pretended anger, dejection, fear, and shame on this account, but should not disobey the mother or nurse at any time.

She should make out to the mother or nurse that the man is suffering from bad health and, making this a pretext for going to see him, she should go on that account. She is, moreover, to do the following things for the purpose of gaining the man's favor, viz.:

Sending her female attendant to bring the flowers used by him on the previous day, in order that she may use them herself as a mark of affection, also asking for the mixture of betel nut and leaves that have remained uneaten by him; expressing wonder at his knowledge of sexual intercourse, and the several means of enjoyment used by him; learning from him the sixty-four kinds of pleasure mentioned by Babhravya; continually practicing the ways of enjoyment as taught by him and according to his liking; keeping his secrets; telling him her own desires and secrets; concealing her anger; never neglecting him on the bed when he turns his face towards her; touching any parts of his body according to his wish; kissing and embracing him when he is asleep; looking at him with apparent anxiety when he is wrapped in thought, or thinking of some subject other than herself; showing neither complete shamelessness, nor excessive bashfulness when he meets her, or sees her standing on the terrace of her house from the public road; hating his enemies; loving those who are dear to him; showing a liking for that which he likes; being in high or low spirits according to the state that he is in himself; expressing a curiosity to see his wives; not continuing her anger for a long time; suspecting even the marks and wounds made by herself with her nails and teeth on his body to have been made by some other woman; keeping her love for him unexpressed by words, but showing it by deeds, and signs, and hints; remaining silent when he is asleep, intoxicated, or sick; being very attentive when he describes his good actions, and reciting them afterwards to his praise and benefit; giving witty replies to him if he be sufficiently attached to her; listening to all his stories except those that relate to her rivals; expressing feelings of dejection and sorrow if he sighs, yawns, or falls down; pronouncing the words "live long" when he sneezes; pretending to be ill, or to have the desire of pregnancy when she feels dejected; abstaining from praising the good qualities of anybody else, and from censuring those who possess the same faults as her own man; wearing anything that may have been given to her by him; abstaining from putting on her ornaments, and from taking food when he is in pain, sick, low-spirited, or suffering from misfortune, and condoling and lamenting with him over the same; wishing to accompany him if he happens to leave the country himself or if he be banished from it by the king; expressing a desire not to live after him; telling him that the whole object and desire of her life was to be united with him;

offering previously promised sacrifices to the Deity when he acquires wealth, or has some desire fulfilled, or when he has recovered from some illness or disease; putting on ornaments every day; not acting too freely with him; reciting his name and the name of his family in her songs; placing his hand on her loin, bosom and forehead, and falling asleep after feeling the pleasure of his touch; sitting on his lap and falling asleep there; wishing to have a child by him; desiring not to live longer than he does; abstaining from revealing his secrets to others; dissuading him from vows and fasts by saying "let the sin fall upon me"; keeping vows and fasts along with him when it is impossible to change his mind on the subject; telling him that vows and fasts are difficult to be observed, even by herself, when she has any dispute with him about them; looking on her own wealth and his without any distinction; abstaining from going to public assemblies without him, and accompanying him when he desires her to do so; taking delight in using things previously used by him, and in eating food that he has left uneaten; venerating his family, his disposition, his skill in the arts, his learning, his caste, his complexion, his native country, his friends, his good qualities, his age, and his sweet temper; asking him to sing, and to do other such-like things, if able to do them; going to him without paying any regard to fear, to cold, to heat, or to rain; saying with regard to the next world that he should be her lover even there; adapting her tastes, disposition and actions to his liking; abstaining from sorcery; disputing continually with her mother on the subject of going to him, and when forcibly taken by her mother to some other place, expressing her desire to die by taking poison, by starving herself to death, by stabbing herself with some weapon, or by hanging herself; and lastly assuring the man of her constancy and love by means of her agents, and receiving money herself, but abstaining from any dispute with her mother with regard to pecuniary matters.

When the man sets out on a journey, she should make him swear that he will return quickly, and in his absence should put aside her vows of worshipping the Deity, and should wear no ornaments except those that are lucky. If the time fixed for his return has passed, she should endeavor to ascertain the real time of his return from omens, from the reports of the people, and from the position of the planets, the moon and the stars. On occasions of amusement and of auspicious dreams, she should wear no ornaments except those that are lucky. If, moreover, she feels melancholy, or sees any inauspicious omen, she should perform some rite to appease the Deity.

When the man does return home, she should worship the god Kama (i.e., the Indian Cupid), and offer oblations to other deities, and having caused a pot filled with water to be brought by her friends, she should perform the worship in honor of the crow who eats the offerings which we make to the names of deceased relations. After the first visit is over, she should ask her lover also to perform certain rites, and this he will do if he is sufficiently attached to her.

Now a man is said to be sufficiently attached to a woman when his love is disinterested; when he has the same object in view as his beloved one; when he is quite free from any suspicions on her account; and when he is indifferent to money with regard to her.

Such is the manner of a courtesan living with a man like a wife, and set forth here for the sake of guidance from the rules of Dattaka. What is not laid down here should be practiced according to the custom of the people, and the nature of each individual man.

There are also two verses on the subject, as follows:

"The extent of the love of women is not known, even to those who are the objects of their affection, on account of its subtlety, and on account of the avarice and natural intelligence of womankind."

"Women are hardly ever known in their true light, though they may love men, or become indifferent toward them; may give them delight, or abandon them; or may extract from them all the wealth that they may possess."

Chapter Three

ON THE MEANS OF GETTING MONEY,
ON THE SIGNS OF THE CHANGE OF A LOVER'S FEELINGS,
AND ON THE WAY TO GET RID OF HIM

Money is got out of a lover in two ways, viz.:

By natural or lawful means, and by artifices. Old authors are of the opinion that when a courtesan can get as much money as she wants from her lover, she should not make use of artifice. But Vatsyayana lays down that, though she may get some money from him by natural means, yet when she makes use of artifice he gives her doubly more, and therefore artifice should be resorted to for the purpose of extorting money from him at all events.

Now the artifices to be used for getting money from the lover are as follows:

1. Taking money from him on different occasions, for the purpose of purchasing various articles such as ornaments, food, drink, flowers, perfumes and clothes, and either not buying them, or getting from him more than their cost.

2. Praising his intelligence to his face.

3. Pretending to be obliged to make gifts on occasions of festivals connected with vows, trees, gardens, temples, or tanks.[1]

4. Pretending that, at the time of going to his house, her jewels have been stolen either by the king's guards or by robbers.

5. Alleging that her property has been destroyed by fire, by the falling of her house, or by the carelessness of servants.

6. Pretending to have lost the ornaments of her lover, along with her own.

7. Causing him to hear through other people of the expenses incurred by her in coming to see him.

8. Contracting debts for the sake of her lover.

9. Disputing with her mother on account of some expense occurred by her for the lover, and which was not approved of by her mother.

10. Not going to parties and festivities in the houses of her friends for the want of presents to make to them, she having previously informed her lover of the valuable presents given to her by these very friends.

11. Not performing certain festive rites under the pretense that she has no money to perform them with.

12. Engaging artists to do something for her lover.

13. Entertaining physicians and ministers for the purpose of attaining some object.

14. Assisting friends and benefactors, both on festive occasions and in misfortune.

15. Performing household rites.

16. Having to pay the expenses of the ceremony of marriage of the son of a female friend.

17. Having to satisfy curious wishes during her state of pregnancy.

18. Pretending to be ill, and charging her cost of treatment.

19. Having to remove the troubles of a friend.

20. Selling some of her ornaments, so as to give her lover a present.

21. Pretending to sell some of her ornaments, furniture, or cooking utensils to a trader, who has been already tutored how to behave in the matter.

22. Having to buy cooking utensils of greater value than those of other people, so that they might be more easily distinguished, and not changed for others of an inferior description.

23. Remembering the former favors of her lover, and causing them always to be spoken of by her friends and followers.

24. Informing her lover of the great gains of other courtesans.

25. Describing before them, and in the presence of her lover, her own great gains, and making them out to be greater even than theirs, though such may not have been really the case.

26. Openly opposing her mother when she endeavors

to persuade her to take up with men with whom she had been formerly acquainted, on account of the great gains to be got from them.

27. Lastly, pointing out to her lover the liberality of his rivals.

Thus end the ways and means of getting money.

A woman should always know the state of the mind, of the feelings, and of the disposition of her lover toward her, from the changes of his temper, his manner, and the color of his face.

The behavior of a waning lover is as follows:

1. He gives the woman either less than is wanted, or something other than that which is asked for.

2. He keeps her in hopes by promises.

3. He pretends to do one thing, and does something else.

4. He does not fulfill her desires.

5. He forgets his promises, or does something other than that which he has promised.

6. He speaks with his own servants in a mysterious way.

7. He sleeps in some other house under the pretense of having to do something for a friend.

8. Lastly, he speaks in private with the attendants of a woman with whom he was formerly acquainted.

Now when a courtesan finds that her lover's disposition toward her is changing, she should get possession of all his best things before he becomes aware of her intentions, and allow a supposed creditor to take them away forcibly from her in satisfaction of some pretended debt. After this, if the lover is rich and has always behaved well toward her, she should ever treat him with respect; but if he is poor and destitute, she should get rid of him as if she had never been acquainted with him in any way before.

The means of getting rid of a lover are as follows:

1. Describing the habits and vices of the lover as disagreeable and censurable, with the sneer of the lip, and the stamp of the foot.

2. Speaking on a subject with which he is not acquainted.

3. Showing no admiration for his learning, and passing a censure upon it.

4. Putting down his pride.

5. Seeking the company of men who are superior to him in learning and wisdom.

6. Showing a disregard for him on all occasions.

7. Censuring men possessed of the same faults as her lover.

8. Expressing dissatisfaction at the ways and means of enjoyment used by him.

9. Not giving him her mouth to kiss.

10. Refusing access to her Jaghana, i.e., the part of the body between the navel and the thighs.

11. Showing a dislike for the wounds made by his nails and teeth.

12. Not pressing close up against him at the time when he embraces her.

13. Keeping her limbs without movement at the time of congress.

14. Desiring him to enjoy her when he is fatigued.

15. Laughing at his attachment to her.

16. Not responding to his embraces.

17. Turning away from him when he begins to embrace her.

18. Pretending to be sleepy.

19. Going out visiting, or into company, when she perceives his desire to enjoy her during the daytime.

20. Misconstruing his words.

21. Laughing without any joke or, at the time of any joke made by him, laughing under some other pretense.

22. Looking with side glances at her own attendants, and clapping her hands when he says anything.

23. Interrupting him in the middle of his stories, and beginning to tell other stories herself.

24. Reciting his faults and his vices, and declaring them to be incurable.

25. Saying words to her female attendants calculated to cut the heart of her lover to the quick.

26. Taking care not to look at him when he comes to her.

27. Asking from him what cannot be granted.

28. And, after all, finally dismissing him.

There are also two verses on the subject, as follows:
"The duty of a courtesan consists in forming connections with suitable men after due and full consideration, and attaching the person with whom she is united to herself; in obtaining wealth from the person who is attached to her, and then dismissing him after she has taken away all his possessions."

"A courtesan leading in this manner the life of a wife is not troubled with too many lovers, and yet obtains an abundance of wealth."

---

[1] On the completion of a vow, a festival takes place. Some trees, such as the Peepul and Banyan trees, are invested with sacred threads like the Brahman's, and on the occasion of this ceremony a festival is given. In the same way when gardens are made, and tanks or temples built, then also festivals are observed.

Chapter Four

ABOUT RE-UNION WITH A FORMER LOVER

When a courtesan abandons her present lover after all his wealth is exhausted, she may then consider about her reunion with a former lover. But she should return to him only if he has acquired fresh wealth, or is still wealthy, and if he is still attached to her. And if this man be living at the time with some other woman, she should consider well before she acts.

Now such a man can only be in one of the six following conditions, viz.:

1. He may have left the first woman of his own accord, and may even have left another woman since then.

2. He may have been driven away from both women.

3. He may have left the one woman of his own accord, and been driven away by the other.

4. He may have left the one woman of his own accord, and be living with another woman.

5. He may have been driven away from the one woman, and left the other of his own accord.

6. He may have been driven away by the one woman, and may be living with another.

(1.) Now if the man has left both women of his own accord, he should not be resorted to, on account of the fickleness of his mind, and his indifference to the excellence of both of them.

(2.) As regards the man who may have been driven away from both women, if he has been driven away from the last one because the woman could get more money from some other man, then he should be resorted to for, if attached to the first woman, he would give her more money through vanity and emulation to spite the other woman. But if he has been driven away by the woman on account of his poverty, or stinginess, he should not then be resorted to.

(3.) In the case of the man who may have left the one woman of his own accord, and been driven away by the other, if he agrees to return to the former and give her plenty of money beforehand, then he should be resorted to.

(4.) In the case of the man who may have left the one woman of his own accord, and be living with another woman, the former (wishing to take up with him again) should first ascertain if he left her in the first instance in the hope of finding some particular excellence in the other woman, and that, not having found any such excellence, he was willing to come back to her, and to give her much money on account of his conduct, and on account of his affection still existing for her.

Or whether, having discovered many faults in the other woman, he would now see even more excellences in herself than actually exist, and would be prepared to give her much money for these qualities.

Or lastly, to consider whether he was a weak man, or a man fond of enjoying many women, or one who liked a poor woman, or one who never did anything for the woman that he was with. After maturely considering all these things, she should resort to him or not, according to circumstances.

(5.) As regards the man who may have been driven away from the one woman, and left the other of his own accord, the former woman (wishing to reunite with him) should first ascertain whether he still has any affection for her, and would consequently spend much money upon her; or whether, being attached to her excellent qualities, he did not take delight in any other women; or whether, being driven away from her formerly before completely satisfying his sexual desires, he wished to get back to her, so as to be revenged for the injury done to him; or whether he wished to create confidence in her mind, and then take back from her the wealth which she formerly took from him and finally destroy her; or lastly, whether he wished first to separate her from her present lover, and then to break away from her himself. If, after considering all these things, she is of the opinion that his intentions are really pure and honest, she can reunite herself with him. But if his mind be at all tainted with evil intentions, he should be avoided.

(6.) In the case of the man who may have been driven away by one woman, and be living with another, if the man makes overtures to return to the first one, the courtesan should consider well before she acts and, while the other woman is engaged in attracting him to herself, she should try in her turn (though keeping herself behind the scenes) to gain him over, on the grounds of any of the following considerations, viz.:

1. That he was driven away unjustly and for no proper reason and, now that he has gone to another woman, every effort must be used to bring him back to myself.

2. That if he were once to converse with me again, he would break away from the other woman.

3. That the pride of my present lover would be put down by means of the former one.

4. That he has become wealthy, has secured a higher position, and holds a place of authority under the king.

5. That he is separate from his wife.

6. That he is now independent.

7. That he lives apart from his father, or brother.

8. That by making peace with him, I shall be able to get hold of a very rich man, who is now prevented from coming to me by my present lover.

9. That, as he is not respected by his wife, I shall now be able to separate him from her.

10. That the friend of this man loves my rival, who hates me cordially; I shall therefore by this means separate the friend from his mistress.

11. And lastly, I shall bring discredit upon him by bringing him back to me, thus showing the fickleness of his mind.

When a courtesan is resolved to take up again with a former lover, her Pithamurda and other servants should tell her that his former expulsion from the woman's house was caused by the wickedness of her mother; that the woman loved him just as much as ever at that time, but could not help the occurence on account of her deference to her mother's will; that she hated the union of her present lover, and disliked him excessively. In addition to this, they should create confidence in his mind by speaking to him of her former lover for him, and should allude to the mark of that love that she has ever remembered. This mark of her love should be connected with some kind of pleasure that may have been practiced by him, such as his way of kissing her, or manner of having connection with her.

Thus end the ways of bringing about a reunion with a former lover.

When a woman has to choose between two lovers, one of whom was formerly united with her, while the other is a stranger, the Acharyas (sages) are of the opinion that the first one is preferable, because his disposition and character being already known by previous careful observation, he can be easily pleased and satisfied; but Vatsyayana thinks that a former lover, having already spent a great deal of his wealth, is not able or willing to give much money again, and is not therefore to be relied upon so much as a stranger. Particular cases may however arise differing from this general rule, on account of the different natures of men.

There are also verses on the subject, as follows:

"Reunion with a former lover may be desirable so as to separate some particular woman from some particular man, or some particular man from some particular woman, or to have a certain effect upon the present lover."

"When a man is excessively attached to a woman, he is afraid of her coming into contact with other men; he does not then regard or notice her faults, and he gives her much wealth through fear of her leaving him."

"A courtesan should be agreeable to the man who is attached to her, and despise the man who does not care for her. If, while living with one man, a messenger comes to her from some other man, she may either refuse to listen to any negotiations on his part, or appoint a fixed time for him to visit her, but she should not leave the man who may be living with her and who may be attached to her."

"A wise woman should only renew her connection with a former lover if she is satisfied that good fortune, gain, love, and friendship are likely to be the result of such a reunion."

Chapter Five

ON DIFFERENT KINDS OF GAIN

When a courtesan is able to realize much money every day, by reason of many customers, she should not confine herself to a single lover; under such circumstances, she should fix her rate for one night, after considering the place, the season, and the condition of the people, also having regard to her own good qualities and good looks, and after comparing her rates with those of other courtesans. She can inform her lovers and friends and acquaintances about these charges. If, however, she can obtain a great gain from a single lover, she may resort to him alone, and live with him like a wife.

Now, the sages are of the opinion that, when a courtesan has the chance of an equal gain from two lovers at the same time, a preference should be given to the one who would give her the kind of thing which she wants. But Vatsyayana says that the preference should be given to the one who gives her gold, because it cannot be taken back like some other things, it can be easily received, and is also the means of procuring anything that may be wished for. Of such things as gold, silver, copper, bell metal, iron, pots, furniture, beds, upper garments, under vestments, fragrant substances, vessels made of gourds, ghee, oil, corn, cattle, and other things of a like nature, the first, viz., gold, is superior to all the others.

When the same labor is required to gain any two lovers, or when the same kind of thing is to be got from each of them, the choice should be made by the advice of a friend, or it can be made from their personal qualities, or from the signs of good or bad fortune that may be connected with them.

When there are two lovers, one of whom is attached to the courtesan, and the other is simply very generous, the sages say that a preference should be given to the generous lover, but Vatsyayana is of the opinion that the one who is really attached to the courtesan should be preferred, because he can be made to be generous, even

as a miser gives money if he becomes fond of a woman, but a man who is simply generous cannot be made to love with real attachment. But among those who are attached to her, if there is one who is poor, and one who is rich, the preference is of course to be given to the latter.

When there are two lovers, one of whom is generous, and the other ready to do any service for the courtesan, some sages say that the one who is ready to do the service should be preferred, but Vatsyayana is of the opinion that a man who does a service thinks that he has gained his object when he has done something once, but a generous man does not care for what he has given before. Even here the choice should be guided by the likelihood of the future good to be derived from her union with either of them.

When one of two lovers is grateful, and the other liberal, some sages say that the liberal one should be preferred, but Vatsyayana is of the opinion that the former should be chosen, because liberal men are generally haughty, plain spoken, and wanting in consideration towards others. Even though these liberal men have been on friendly terms for a long time, yet if they see any fault in the courtesan, or are told lies about her by some other woman, they do not care for past services, but leave abruptly. On the other hand, the grateful man does not at once break off from her, on account of a regard for the pains she may have taken to please him. In this case also, the choice is to be guided with regard to what may happen in the future.

When an occasion for complying with the request of a friend, and a chance of getting money come together, the sages say that the chance of getting money should be preferred. But Vatsyayana thinks that money can be obtained tomorrow as well as today, but if the request of a friend be not at once complied with, he may become disaffected. Even here, in making the choice, regard must be paid to future good fortune.

On such an occasion, however, the courtesan might

pacify her friend by pretending to have some work to do, and telling him that his request will be complied with next day, and in this way secure the chance of getting the money that has been offered her.

When the chance of getting money, and the chance of avoiding some disaster come at the same time, the sages are of the opinion that the chance of getting money should be preferred, but Vatsyayana says that money has only a limited importance, while a disaster that is once averted may never occur again. Here, however, the choice should be guided by the greatness or smallness of the disaster.

The gains of the wealthiest and best kind of courtesans are to be spent as follows:

Building temples, tanks, and gardens; giving a thousand cows to different Brahmans; carrying on the worship of the Gods, and celebrating festivals in their honor; and, lastly, performing such vows as may be within their means.

The gains of other courtesans are to be spent as follows:

Having a white dress to wear every day; getting sufficient food and drink to satisfy hunger and thirst; eating daily a perfumed Tambula, i.e., a mixture of betel nut and betel leaves; and wearing ornaments gilt with gold. The ages say that these represent the gains of all the middle and lower classes of courtesans, but Vatsyayana is of the opinion that their gains cannot be calculated, or fixed in any way, as these depend on the influences of the place, the customs of the people, their own appearance, and many other things.

When a courtesan wants to keep some particular man from some other woman; or wishes to get him away from some woman to whom he may be attached; or to deprive some woman of the gains realized by her from him; or if she thinks that she would raise her position; or enjoy some great fortune; or become desirable to all men by uniting herself with this man; or if she wishes to get his assistance in averting some misfortune; or is really attached to him and loves him; or wishes to injure somebody through this means; or has regard to some former favor conferred upon her by him; or wishes to be united with him merely from desire; for any of the above reasons, she should agree to take from him only a small sum of money in a friendly way.

When a courtesan intends to abandon a particular lover and take up with another one; or when she has reason to believe that her lover will shortly leave her, and return to his wives; or that, having squandered all his money, and become penniless, his guardian, or master, or father would come and take him away; or that her lover is about to lose his position; or lastly, that he is of a very fickle mind; she should, under any of these circumstances, endeavor to get as much money as she can from him as soon as possible.

On the other hand, when the courtesan thinks that her lover is about to receive valuable presents; or get a place of authority from the king; or be near the time of inheriting a fortune; or that his ship would soon arrive laden with merchandise; or that he has large stocks of corn and other commodities; or that if anything was done for him it would not be done in vain; or that he is always true to his word; then should she have regard to her future welfare, and live with the man like a wife.

There are also verses on the subjects, as follows:

"In considering her present gains, and her future welfare, a courtesan should avoid such persons as have gained their means of subsistence with very great difficulty, as also those who have become selfish and hard-hearted by becoming the favorites of kings."

"She should make every endeavor to unite herself with prosperous and well-to-do people, and with those which it is dangerous to avoid, or to slight in any way. Even at some cost to herself she should become acquainted with energetic and liberal-minded men, who when pleased would give her a large sum of money, even for very little service, or for some small thing."

Chapter Six

ON GAINS AND LOSSES,
ATTENDANT GAINS AND LOSSES AND DOUBTS;
ALSO ON THE DIFFERENT KINDS OF COURTESANS

It sometimes happens that, while gains are being sought for, or expected to be realized, that losses only are the result of our efforts. The causes of these losses are:

Weakness of intellect
Excessive love
Excessive pride
Excessive self-conceit
Excessive simplicity
Excessive confidence
Excessive anger
Carelessness
Recklessness
Influence of evil genius
Accidental circumstances

The results of these losses are:
Expense incurred without any result
Destruction of future good fortune
Stoppage of gains about to be realized
Loss of what is already obtained
Acquisition of a sour temper
Becoming unaimiable to everybody
Injury to head
Loss of hair, and other accidents

Now, gain is of three kinds, viz.: gain of wealth, gain of religious merit, and gain of pleasure; and similarly, loss is of three kinds, viz.: loss of wealth, loss of religious merit, and loss of pleasure. At the time when gains are sought for, if other gains come along with them, these are called attendant gains. When gain is uncertain, the doubt of its being a gain is called a simple doubt. When there is a doubt whether either of two things will happen or not, it is called a mixed doubt. If while one thing is being done two results take place, it is called a combination of two results, and if several results follow from the same action, it is called a combination of results on every side.

We shall now give examples of the above.

As already stated, gain is of three kinds, and loss, which is opposed to gain, is also of three kinds.

(a). When by living with a great man a courtesan acquires present wealth, and in addition to this becomes acquainted with other people, and thus obtains a chance of future fortune and an accession of wealth, and becomes desirable to all, this is called a gain of wealth attended by other gain.

(b). When by living with a man a courtesan simply gets money, this is called a gain of wealth not attended by any other gain.

(c). When a courtesan receives money from other people besides her lover, the results are: the chance of the loss of future good from her present lover; the chance of disaffection of a man securely attached to her; the hatred of all; and the chance of a union with some low person tending to destroy her future good. This gain is called a gain of wealth attended by losses.

(d). When a courtesan at her own expense, and without any results in the shape of gain, has connection with a great man, or an avaricious minister for the sake of diverting some misfortune, or removing some cause that may be threatening the destruction of a great gain, this loss is said to be a loss of wealth attended by gains of the future good which it may bring about.

(e). When a courtesan is kind, even at her own expense to a man who is very stingy, or to a man proud of his looks, or to an ungrateful man skilled in gaining the heart of others, without any good resulting from these connections to her in the end, this loss is called a loss of wealth not attended by any gain.

(f). When a courtesan is kind to any such men as described above, but who in addition are favorites of the king, and moreover cruel and powerful, without any good result in the end, and with a chance of her being turned away at any moment, this loss is called a loss of wealth attended by other losses.

In this way gains and losses, and attendant gains and losses in religious merit and in pleasures may become known to the reader, and combinations of all of them may also be made.

Thus end the remarks on gains and losses, and attendant gains and losses.

In the next place we come to doubts, which are again of three kinds, viz.: doubts about wealth, doubts about religious merit, and doubts about pleasures.

The following are examples.

(a). When a courtesan is not certain how much a man may give her, or spend upon her, this is called a doubt about wealth.

(b). When a courtesan feels doubtful whether she is right in entirely abandoning a lover from whom she is unable to get money, she having taken all his wealth from him in the first instance, this doubt is called a doubt about religious merit.

(c). When a courtesan is unable to get hold of a lover to her liking, and is uncertain whether she will derive any pleasure from a person surrounded by his family, or from a low person, this is called a doubt about pleasure.

(d). When a courtesan is uncertain whether some powerful but low-principled fellow would cause loss to her on account of her being civil to him, this is called a doubt about the loss of wealth.

(e). When a courtesan feels doubtful whether she would lose religious merit by abandoning a man who is attached to her without giving him the slightest favor, and thereby causing him unhappiness in this world and the next,[1] this doubt is called a doubt about the loss of religious merit.

(f). When a courtesan is uncertain as to whether she might create disaffection by speaking out, and revealing her love, and thus not get her desire satisfied, this is called a doubt about the loss of pleasure.

Thus end the remarks on doubts.

Mixed Doubts

(a). The intercourse or connection with a stranger, whose disposition is unknown, and who may have been introduced by a lover, or by one who possessed authority, may be productive either of gain or loss, and therefore this is called a mixed doubt about the gain and loss of wealth.

(b). When a courtesan is requested by a friend, or is impelled by pity to have intercourse with a learned Brahman, a religious student, a sacrificer, a devotee, or an ascetic who may have all fallen in love with her, and who may be consequently at the point of death, by doing this she might either gain or lose religious merit, and therefore this is called a mixed doubt about the gain or loss of religious merit.

(c). If a courtesan relies solely upon the report of other people (i.e., hearsay) about a man, and goes to him without ascertaining herself whether he possesses good qualities or not, she may either gain or lose pleasure in proportion as he may be good or bad, and therefore this is called a mixed doubt about the gain and loss of pleasure.

Uddalika has described the gains and losses on both sides as follows:

(a). If, when living with a lover, a courtesan gets both wealth and pleasure from him, it is called a gain on both sides.

(b). When a courtesan lives with a lover at her own expense without getting any profit out of it, and the lover even takes back from her what he may have formerly given her, it is called a loss on both sides.

(c). When a courtesan is uncertain whether a new acquaintance would become attached to her, and, moreover, if he becomes attached to her, whether he would give her anything, it is called a doubt on both sides about gains.

(d). When a courtesan is uncertain whether a former enemy, if made up to by her at her own expense, would do her some injury on account of his grudge against her; or, if becoming attached to her, would take away angrily from her anything that he may have given to her, this is called a doubt on both sides about loss.

Babhravya has described the gains and losses on both sides as follows.

(a). When a courtesan has to incur further expense if she goes to see a man, and yet runs the risk of incurring an irremediable loss if she does not go to see him, this is called a loss on both sides.

(c). When a courtesan is uncertain, whether a particular man would give her anything on her going to see him, without incurring expense on her part, or whether on her neglecting him another man would give her something, this is called a doubt on both sides about gain.

(d). When a courtesan is uncertain whether, on going at her own expense to see an old enemy, he would take back from her what he may have given her, or whether by her not going to see him he would cause some disaster to fall upon her, this is called a doubt on both sides about loss.

By combining the above, the following six kinds of mixed results are produced, viz.:

(a). Gain on one side, and loss on the other.

(b). Gain on one side, and doubt of gain on the other.

(c). Gain on one side, and doubt of loss on the other.

(d). Loss on one side, and doubt of gain on the other.

(e). Doubt of gain on one side, and doubt of loss on the other.

(f). Doubt of loss on one side, and loss on the other.

A courtesan, having considered all the above things and

taken counsel with her friends, should act so as to acquire gain, the chances of great gain, and the warding off of any great disaster. Religious merit and pleasure should also be formed into separate combinations like those of wealth, and then all should be combined with each other, so as to form new combinations.

When a courtesan consorts with men, she should cause each of them to give her money as well as pleasure. At particular times, such as the Spring Festivals, etc., she should make her mother announce to the various men that on a certain day her daughter would remain with the man who would gratify such and such a desire of hers.

When young men approach her with delight, she should think of what she may accomplish through them.

The combination of gains and losses on all sides are: gain on one side and loss on all others; loss on one side and gain on all others; gain on all sides; and loss on all sides.

A courtesan should also consider doubts about gain and doubt about loss with reference both to wealth, religious merit, and pleasure.

Thus ends the consideration of gain, loss, attendant gains, attendant losses, and doubts.

The different kinds of courtesans are:
A bawd
A female attendant
An unchaste woman
A dancing girl
A female artisan
A woman who has left her family
A woman living on her beauty
And, finally, a regular courtesan.

All the above kinds of courtesans are acquainted with various kinds of men, and should consider the ways of getting money from them, or pleasing them, of separating themselves from them, and of re-uniting with them. They should also take into consideration particular gains and losses, attendant gains and losses, and doubts in accordance with their several conditions.

Thus ends the consideration of courtesans.

There are also two verses on the subject, as follows:
"Men want pleasure, while women want money, and therefore this Part, which treats of the means of gaining wealth, should be studied."

"There are some women who seek for love, and there are others who seek for money; for the former the ways of love are told in previous portions of this work, while the ways of getting money, as practiced by courtesans, are described in this Part."

[1] The souls of men who die with their desire unfulfilled are said to go to the world of the Manes, and not directly to the Supreme Spirit.

Part Seven

On the Means of Attracting Others to One's Self

Chapter One

ON PERSONAL ADORNMENT, ON SUBJUGATING THE HEARTS OF OTHERS, AND ON TONIC MEDICINES

When a person fails to obtain the object of his desires by any of the ways previously related, he should then have recourse to other ways of attracting others to himself.

Now, good looks, good qualities, youth, and liberality are the chief and most natural means of making a person agreeable in the eyes of others. But in the absence of these, a man or woman must have resort to artificial means, or to art, and the following are some recipes that may be found useful.

(a). An ointment made of the *Tabernamontana coronaria*, the *Costus speciosus* or *arabicus*, and the *Flacourtia cataphracta*, can be used as an unguent of adornment.

(b). If a fine powder is made of the above plants, and applied to the wick of a lamp, which is made to burn with the oil of blue vitriol, the black pigment or lamp black produced therefrom, when applied to the eyelashes, has the effect of making a person look lovely.

(c). The oil of the hogweed, the *Echites putescens*, the sarina plant, the yellow amaranth, and the leaf of the nymphae, if applied to the body, has the same effect.

(d). A black pigment from the same plants produces a similar effect.

(e). By eating the powder of the *Nelumbrium speciosum*, the blue lotus, and the *Mesna roxburghii*, with ghee and honey, a man becomes lovely in the eyes of others.

(f). The above things, together with the *Tabernamontana coronaria*, and the *Xanthochymus pictorius*, if used as an ointment, produce the same results.

(g). If the bone of a peacock or of a hyena be covered with gold, and tied on the right hand, it makes a man lovely in the eyes of other people.

(h). In the same way, if a bead made of the seed of the jujube or of the conch shell be enchanted by the incantations mentioned in the Atharvana Veda, or by the incantations of those well skilled in the science of magic, and tied on the hand, it produces the same result as described above.

(i). When a female attendant arrives at the age of puberty, her master should keep her secluded and, when men ardently desire her on account of her seclusion, and on account of the difficulty of approaching her, he should then bestow her hand on such a person as may endow her with wealth and happiness.

This is a means of increasing the loveliness of a person in the eyes of others.

In the same way, when the daughter of a courtesan arrives at the age of puberty, the mother should get together a lot of young men of the same age, disposition, and knowledge of her daughter, and tell them that she would give her in marriage to the person who would give her presents of a particular kind.

After this, the daughter should be kept in seclusion as far as possible, and the mother should give her in marriage to the man who may be ready to give her the presents agreed upon. If the mother is unable to get so much out of the man, she should show some of her own things as having been given to the daughter by the bridegroom.

Or, the mother may allow her daughter to be married to the man privately, as if she were ignorant of the whole affair, and then, pretending that it has come to her knowledge, she may give her consent to the union.

The daughter, too, should make herself attractive to the sons of wealthy citizens, unknown to her mother, and make them attached to her, and for this purpose should meet them at the time of learning to sing, and in places where music is played, and at the houses of other people, and then request her mother, through a female friend or servant, to be allowed to unite herself to the man who is most agreeable to her.[1]

When the daughter of a courtesan is thus given to a man, the ties of marriage should be observed for one year, and after that she may do what she likes. But even after the end of the year, when otherwise engaged, if she should be now and then invited by her first husband to come and see him, she should put aside her present gain, and go to him for the night.

Such is the mode of temporary marriage among courtesans, and of increasing their loveliness, and their value in the eyes of others. What has been said about them should also be understood to apply to the daughters of dancing women, whose mothers should give them only to such persons as are likely to become useful to them in various ways.

Thus end the ways of making oneself lovely in the eyes of others.

(a). If a man, after annointing his lingam with a mixture of the powders of the white thorn apple, the long pepper, the black pepper, and honey, engages in sexual union with a woman, he makes her subject to his will.

(b). The application of a mixture of the leaf of the plant vatodbhranta, of the flowers thrown on a human corpse when carried out to be burnt, and of the powder of the bones of the peacock, and of the jiwanjiva bird produces the same effect.

(c). The remains of a kite who has died a natural death, ground into powder and mixed with cowach and honey, has also the same effect.

(d). Annointing oneself with an ointment made of the plant *Emblica myrabolens* has the power of subjecting women to one's will.

(e). If a man cuts into small pieces the sprouts of the vajnasunhi plant, and dips them into a mixture of red arsenic and sulphur, and then dries them seven times, and applies this powder mixed with honey to his lingam, he can subjugate a woman to his will directly that he has had sexual union with her, or if, by burning these very sprouts at night and looking at the smoke, he sees a golden moon behind, he will then be successful with any woman; or if he throws some of the powder of these same sprouts mixed with the excrement of a monkey upon a maiden, she will not be given in marriage to anybody else.

(f). If pieces of the arris root are dressed with the oil of the mango, and placed for six months in a hole made in the trunk of the sisu tree, and are then taken out and made up into an ointment, and applied to the lingam, this is said to serve as the means of subjugating women.

(g). If the bone of a camel is dipped into the juice of the plant *Eclipta prostata*, and then burnt, and the black pigment produced from its ashes is placed in a box also made of the bone of a camel, and applied together with antimony to the eyelashes with a pencil also made of the bone of a camel, then that pigment is said to be very pure, and wholesome for the eyes, and serves as a means of

subjugating others to the person who uses it. The same effect can be produced by black pigment made of the bones of hawks, vultures, and peacock.

Thus end the ways of subjugating others to one's own will.

Now the means of increasing sexual vigor are as follows:

(a). A man obtains sexual vigor by drinking milk mixed with sugar, the root of the uchchata plant, the pipar chaba, and licorice.

(b). Drinking milk mixed with sugar, and having the testicle of a ram or goat boiled in it, is also productive of vigor.

(c). The drinking of the juice of the *Hedysarum gangeticum*, the kuili, and the kshirika plant mixed with milk, produces the same effect.

(d). The seed of long pepper along with the seeds of the *Sanseviera roxburghiana* and the *Hedysarum gangeticum* plant, all pounded together and mixed with milk, is productive of a similar result.

(e). According to ancient authors, if a man pounds the seeds or roots of the *Trapa bispinosa*, the kasurika, the tuscan jasmine, and licorice, together with the kshira-kapoli (a kind of onion), and puts the powder into milk mixed with sugar and ghee and, having boiled the whole mixture on a moderate fire, drinks the paste so formed, he will be able to enjoy innumerable women.

(f). In the same way, if a man mixes rice with the eggs of the sparrow and, having boiled this in milk, adds to it ghee and honey, and drinks as much of it as is necessary, this will produce the same effect.

(g). If a man takes the outer covering of sesamum seeds and soaks them with the eggs of sparrows, and then, having boiled them in milk mixed with sugar and ghee, along with the fruits of the *Trapa bispinosa* and the kasurik plant, and adding to it the flour of wheat and beans, and then drinks this composition, he is said to be able to enjoy many women.

(h). If ghee, honey, sugar and licorice in equal quantities, the juice of the fennel plant, and milk are mixed together, this nectar-like composition is said to be holy, and provocative of sexual vigor, a preservative of life, and sweet to the taste.

(i). The drinking of a paste composed of the *Asparagus rasemosus*, the shvadaushtra plant, the guduchi plant, the long pepper, and licorice, boiled in milk, honey, and ghee, in the spring, is said to have the same effect as the above.

(j). Boiling the *Asparagus racemosus* and the shvadaushtra plant, along with the pounded fruits of the *Premna spinosa* in water, and drinking the same, is said to act in the same way.

(k). Drinking boiled ghee, or clarified butter, in the morning during the spring season, is said to be beneficial to health and strength, and agreeable to the taste.

(l). If the powder of the seed of the shvadaustra plant and the flour of barley are mixed together in equal parts, and a portion of it, *i.e.*, two palas in weight, is eaten every morning on getting up, it has the same effect as the preceding recipe.

There are also verses on the subject, as follows:

"The means[2] of producing love and sexual vigor should be learned from the science of medicine, from the Vedas, from those who are learned in the arts of magic, and from confidential relatives. No means should be tried which are doubtful in their effects, which are likely to cause injury to the body, which involve the death of animals, and which bring us in contact with impure things. Such means should only be used as are holy, acknowledged to be good, and approved of by Brahmans, and friends."

[1] It is a custom of the courtesans of Oriental countries to give their daughters temporarily in marriage when they come of age, and after they have received an education in the Kama Sutra and other arts. Full details are given of this at page 76 of "Early Ideas, a group of Hindoo stories collected and collated by Anaryap." W.H. Allen and Co., London, 1881.

[2] From the earliest times, Oriental authors have occupied themselves about aphrodisiacs. The following note on the subject is taken from page 29 of a translation of the Hindu Art of Love, otherwise the Anunga Runga alluded to in the preface of this work, Part I: "Most Eastern treatises divide aphrodisiacs into two different kinds: 1. the mechanical or natural, such as scarification, flagellation, etc.; and 2. the medicinal or artificial. To the former belong the application of insects, as is practiced by some savage races; and all orientalists will remember the tale of the old Brahman whose young wife insisted upon his being again stung by a wasp."

Chapter Two

ON THE WAYS OF EXCITING DESIRE, AND MISCELLANEOUS EXPERIMENTS AND RECIPES

If a man is unable to satisfy a Hastini, or elephant woman, he should have recourse to various means to excite her passion. At the commencement he should rub her yoni with his hand or fingers, and not begin to have intercourse with her until she becomes excited, or experiences pleasure. This is one way of exciting a woman.

Or, he may make use of certain Apadravyas, or things which are put on or around the lingam to supplement its length or thickness, so as to fit it to the yoni. In the opinion of Babhravya, these Apadravyas should be made of gold, silver, copper, iron, ivory, buffalo's horn, various kinds of wood, tin or lead, and should be soft, cool, provocative of sexual vigor, and well fitted to serve the intended purpose. Vatsyayana, however, says that they may be made according to the natural liking of each individual.

The following are the different kinds of Apadravyas.

(1). "The armlet" (Valaya) should be of the same size as the lingam, and should have its outer surface made rough with globules.

(2). "The couple" (Sanghati) is formed of two armlets.

(3). "The bracelet" (Chudaka) is made by joining three or more armlets, until they come up to the required length of the lingam.

(4). "The single bracelet" is formed by wrapping a single wire around the lingam, according to its dimensions.

(5). The Kantuka or Jalaka is a tube open at both ends, with a hole through it, outwardly rough and studded with soft globules, and made to fit the size of the yoni, and tied to the waist.

When such a thing cannot be obtained, then a tube made of the wood apple, or tubular stalk of the bottle gourd, or a reed made soft with oil and extracts of plants, and tied to the waist with string, may be made use of, as also a row of soft pieces of wood tied together.

The above are the things that can be used in connection with, or in the place of, the lingam.

The people of the southern countries think that true sexual pleasure cannot be obtained without perforating the lingam, and they therefore cause it to be pierced like the lobes of the ears of an infant pierced for earrings.

Now, when a young man perforates his lingam, he should pierce it with a sharp instrument, and then stand in water so long as the blood continues to flow. At night he should engage in sexual intercourse, even with vigor, so as to clean the hole. After this he should continue to wash the hole with decoctions, and increase the size by putting into it small pieces of cane, and the *Wrightia antidysenterica*, thus gradually enlarging the orifice. It may also be washed with licorice mixed with honey, and the size of the hole increased by the fruit stalks of the sima-patra plant. The hole should also be anointed with a small quantity of oil.

In the hole made in the lingam a man may put Apadravyas of various forms, such as the "round," the "round on one side," the "wooden mortar," the "flower," the "armlet," the "collection of eight balls," the "lock of hair," the "place where four roads meet," and other things named according to their forms and means of using them. All these Apadravyas should be rough on the outside according to their requirements.

The ways of enlarging the lingam must be now related.

When a man wishes to enlarge his lingam, he should rub it with the bristles of certain insects that live in trees, and then, after rubbing it for ten nights with oils, he should again rub it with the bristles as before. By continuing to do this a swelling will be gradually produced in the lingam, and he should then lie on a cot and cause his lingam to hang down through a hole in the cot. After this he should take away all the pain from the swelling by using cool concoctions. The swelling, which is called "Suka" and is often brought about among the people of the Dravida country, lasts for life.

If the lingam is rubbed with the following things, viz., the plant *Physalis flexuosa,* the shavara-kandaka plant, the jalasuka plant, the fruit of the egg plant, the butter of a she-buffalo, the hasti-charma plant, and the juice of the vajrarasa plant, a swelling lasting for one month will be produced.

By rubbing it with oil boiled in the concoctions of the above things, the same effect will be produced, but lasting for six months.

The enlargement of the lingam is also affected by rubbing it or moistening it with oil boiled on a moderate fire, along with the seeds of the pomegranate and the cucumber, the juices of the vaiuka plant, the hasti-charma plant, and the eggplant.

In addition to the above, other means may be learned from experience and confidential persons.

The miscellaneous experiments and recipes are as follows:

(a). If a man mixes the powder of the milk hedge plant and the kantaka plant with the excrement of a monkey and the powdered root of the lanjalika plant, and throws this mixture on a woman, she will not love anybody else afterwards.

(b). If a man thickens the juice of the fruits of the *Cassia fistula* and the *Eugenia jambolana* by mixing them with the powder of the soma plant, the *Vernonia anthelmintica,* the *Eclipta prostata,* and the lohopa-jihirka, and applies this composition to the yoni of a woman, and then has sexual intercourse with her, his love for her will be destroyed.

(c). The same effect is produced if a man has connection with a woman who has bathed in the buttermilk of a she-buffalo mixed with the powders of the gopalika plant, the banupadika plant, and the yellow amaranth.

(d). An ointment made of the flowers of the *Nauclea cadamba,* the hog plum, and the *Eugenia jambolana,* and used by a woman, causes her to be disliked by her husband.

(e). Garlands made of the above flowers, when worn by the woman, produce the same effect.

(f). An ointment made of the fruit of the *Asteracantha longifolia* (kokilaksha) will contract the yoni of a Hastini or elephant woman, and this contraction lasts for one night.

(g). An ointment made by pounding the roots of the *Nelumbrium speciosum,* and of the blue lotus, and the powder of the plant *Physalis flexuosa* mixed with ghee and honey, will enlarge the yoni of the Mrigi or deer woman.

(h). An ointment made of the fruit of the *Emblica myrabolans* soaked in the milky juice of the milk hedge plant, of the soma plant, the *Calotropis gigantea,* and the juice of the fruit of the *Vernonia anthelmintica,* will make the hair white.

(i). The juice of the roots of the madayantaka plant, the yellow amaranth, the anjanika plant, the *Clitoria ternateea,* and the shlakshnaparni plant, used as a lotion, will make the hair grow.

(j). An ointment made by boiling the above roots in oil, and rubbed in, will make the hair black, and will also gradually restore hair that has fallen off.

(k). If lac is saturated seven times in the sweat of the testicle of a white horse, and applied to a red lip, the lip will become white.

(l). The color of the lips can be regained by means of the madayantika and other plants mentioned above under (i).

(m). A woman who hears a man playing on a reed pipe which has been dressed with the juices of the bahupadika plant, the *Tabernamontana coronaria,* the *Costus speciosus* or *arabicus,* the *Pinus deodora,* the *Euphorbia antiquorum,* the vajra and the kantaka plant, becomes his slave.

(n). If food be mixed with the fruit of the thorn apple (Dathura), it causes intoxication.

(o). If water be mixed with oil and the ashes of any kind of grass except the kusha grass, it becomes the color of milk.

(p). If yellow myrabolans, the hog plum, the shrawana plant, and the priyangu plant be all pounded together, and applied to iron pots, these pots become red.

(q). If a lamp, trimmed with oil extracted from the shrawana and priyangu plants, its wick being made of cloth and the slough of the skins of snakes, is lighted, and long pieces of wood placed near it, those pieces of wood will resemble so many snakes.

(r). Drinking the milk of a white cow who has a white calf at her foot is auspicious, produces fame, and preserves life.

(s). The blessings of venerable Brahmans, well propitiated, have the same effect.

There are also some verses in conclusion:

"Thus have I written in a few words the "Science of love," after reading the texts of ancient authors, and following the ways of enjoyment mentioned in them."

"He who is acquainted with the true principles of this science pays regard to Dharma, Artha, Kama, and to his own experiences, as well as to the teachings of others, and does not act simply on the dictates of his own desire. As for the errors in the science of love which I have mentioned in this work, on my own authority as an author, I have, immediately after mentioning them, carefully censured and prohibited them."

"An act is never looked upon with indulgence for the simple reason that it is authorized by the science, because it ought to be remembered that it is the intention of the science, that the rules which it contains should only be acted upon in particular cases. After reading and

considering the works of Babhravya and other ancient authors, and thinking over the meaning of the rules given by them, the Kama Sutra was composed, according to the precepts of Holy Writ, for the benefit of the world, by Vatsyayana, while leading the life of a religious student, and wholly engaged in the contemplation of the Deity."

"This work is not intended to be used merely as an instrument for satisfying our desires. A person acquainted with the true principles of this science, and who preserves his Dharma, Artha, and Kama, and has regard for the practices of the people, is sure to obtain the mastery over his senses."

"In short, an intelligent and prudent person attending to Dharma and Artha, and attending to Kama also, without becoming the slave of his passions, obtains success in everything that he may undertake."

CONCLUDING REMARKS

Thus end, in seven parts, the Kama Sutra of Vatsyayana, which might otherwise be called a treatise on men and women, their mutual relationship, and connection with each other.

It is a work that should be studied by all, both old and young; the former will find in it real truths, gathered by experience, and already tested by themselves; while the latter will derive the great advantage of learning things, which some perhaps may otherwise never learn at all, or which they may only learn when it is too late ("too late"—those immortal words of Mirabeau) to profit by the learning.

It can also be fairly commended to the student of social science and of humanity, and above all to the student of those early ideas, which have gradually filtered down through the sands of time, and which seem to prove that the human nature of today is much the same as the human nature of the long ago.

It has been said of Balzac (the great, if not the greatest, French novelist) that he seemed to have inherited a natural and intuitive perception of the feelings of men and women, and has described them with an analysis worthy of a man of science. The author of the present work must also have had a considerable knowledge of the humanities. Many of his remarks are so full of simplicity and truth that they have stood the test of time, and stand out still as clear and true as when they were first written, some eighteen hundred years ago.

As a collection of facts, told in plain and simple language, it must be remembered that in those early days there was apparently no idea of embellishing the work, either with a literary style, a flow of language, or a quantity of superfluous padding. The author tells the world what he knows in very concise language, without any attempt to produce an interesting story. From his facts, how many novels could be written! Indeed, much of the matter contained in Parts III, IV, V and VI has formed the basis of many of the stories and the tales of past centuries.

There will be found in Part VII some curious recipes. Many of them appear to be as primitive as the book itself, but in later works of the same nature these recipes and prescriptions have increased, both as regards to quality and to quantity. In the Anunga Runga of "The Stage of Love" mentioned in the Preface in Part I, there are found no fewer than thirty-three different subjects for which one hundred and thirty recipes and prescriptions are given.

As the details may be interesting, these subjects are described as follows:

1. For hastening the paroxysm of the woman.
2. For delaying the orgasm of the man.
3. Aphrodisiacs.
4. For thickening and enlarging the lingam, rendering it sound and strong, hard and lusty.
5. For narrowing and contracting the yoni.
6. For perfuming the yoni.
7. For removing and destroying the hair of the body.
8. For removing the sudden stopping of the monthly ailment.
9. For abating the immoderate appearance of the monthly ailment.
10. For purifying the womb.
11. For causing pregnancy.
12. For preventing miscarriage and other accidents.
13. For ensuring easy labor and ready deliverance.
14. For limiting the number of children.
15. For thickening and beautifying the hair.
16. For obtaining a good black color to it.
17. For whitening and bleaching it.
18. For renewing it.
19. For clearing the skin of the face from eruptions that break out and leave black spots upon it.
20. For removing the black color of the epidermis.

21. For enlarging the breasts of women.

22. For raising and hardening pendulous breasts.

23. For giving a fragrance to the skin.

24. For removing the evil savor of perspiration.

25. For anointing the body after bathing.

26. For causing a pleasant smell to the breath.

27. Drugs and charms for the purposes of fascinating, overcoming, and subduing either men or women.

28. Recipes for enabling a woman to attract and preserve her husband's love.

29. Magical collyriums for winning love and friendship.

30. Prescriptions for reducing other persons to submission.

31. Philters, pills, and other charms.

32. Fascinating incense, or fumigation.

33. Magical verses which have the power of fascination.

Of the one hundred and thirty recipes given, many of them are absurd, but not more perhaps than many of the recipes and prescriptions in use in Europe not so very long ago. Love philters, charms, and herbal remedies have been, in early days, as freely used in Europe as in Asia, and doubtless some people believe in them still in many places.

And now, one word about the author of the work, the good old sage Vatsyayana. It is much to be regretted that nothing can be discovered about his life, his belongings, and his surroundings. At the end of Part VII he states that he wrote the work while leading the life of a religious student (probably at Benares), and while wholly engaged in the contemplation of the Deity. He must have arrived at a certain age at that time, for throughout he gives us the benefit of his experience and his opinions, and these bear the stamp of age rather than of youth; indeed the work could hardly have been written by a young man.

In a beautiful verse of the Vedas of the Christians, it has been said of the peaceful dead that they rest from their labors, and that their works do follow them. Yes, indeed, the works of men of genius do follow them, and remain as a lasting treasure. And though there may be disputes and discussions about the immortality of the body or the soul, nobody can deny the immortality of genius, which ever remains as a bright and guiding star to the struggling humanities of succeeding ages. This work, then, which has stood the test of centuries, has placed Vatsyayana among the immortals, and on This, and on Him, no better elegy or eulogy can be written than the following lines:

"So long as lips shall kiss, and eyes shall see,
So long lives This, and This gives life to Thee."